Building Web Applications with Flask

Use Python and Flask to build amazing web applications, just the way you want them!

Italo Maia

BIRMINGHAM - MUMBAI

Building Web Applications with Flask

First published: June 2015

Production reference: 1240615

Published by Packt Publishing Ltd.
Livery Place
35 Livery Street
Birmingham B3 2PB, UK.

ISBN 978-1-78439-615-2

www.packtpub.com

Credits

Author
Italo Maia

Reviewers
Glenn ten Cate
Michel Henrique Aquino Santos

Commissioning Editor
Nadeem N. Bagban

Acquisition Editor
Harsha Bharwani

Content Development Editor
Shubhangi Dhamgaye

Technical Editor
Shruti Rawool

Copy Editors
Stephen Copestake
Swati Priya

Project Coordinator
Bijal Patel

Proofreader
Safis Editing

Indexer
Mariammal Chettiyar

Production Coordinator
Nilesh R. Mohite

Cover Work
Nilesh R. Mohite

About the Author

Italo Maia is a full-stack developer with 10 years of experience in creating software for the mobile, Web, and desktop environments, having dedicated most of the last few years to development with Python and web technologies.

Author of Flask-Empty, a popular skeleton for Flask projects that aggregates good practices and recipes for quick prototyping, he is active in the Brazilian Python communities, having open source tools and libraries available in GitHub and Bitbucket.

Building Web Applications with Flask is a book written with the invaluable support of families — the Packt family, where I give special thanks to Shubhangi for her dedication and patience with puny little me, and my own family, who so tenderly have looked out for me in my time of need.

About the Reviewers

Glenn ten Cate has over 10 years of experience in the field of security as a coder, hacker, speaker, trainer, and security researcher. He is currently employed as a security engineer at Schuberg Philis in the Netherlands, and has been a speaker at multiple security conferences. His goal is to create an open source software development life cycle approach with the tools and knowledge gathered over the years.

Michel Henrique Aquino Santos is a software engineer with Gravity4. A Brazilian from Belo Horizonte, Minas Gerais, he is 26 years old. He graduated in computer science from the Federal University of Lavras (UFLA) in 2012.

He worked with the research department at the university for 2 years, developing artificial intelligence algorithms to solve optimization problems.

At the end of the course, he joined Tbit and started developing image processing algorithms using C#.

After his graduation, he joined SYDLE and worked with ASP.NET Web Forms using C#, JavaScript, and the MS SQL Server database. After that, he worked with Delphi and the MS SQL server database at Sociedade Mineira de Cultura.

In January 2014, he joined Ezlike, a start-up focused on creating, managing, and optimizing Facebook ads. In April 2015, Ezlike was acquired by the US-based company Gravity4 in order to incorporate a number of other tools focused on digital marketing. There, he works with ASP.NET MVC, JavaScript, AngularJS, KnockoutJS, MongoDB, MS SQL Server, and Cassandra using the Facebook Ads API.

He is also about to begin some personal projects using Python and developing for Android.

www.PacktPub.com

Support files, eBooks, discount offers, and more

For support files and downloads related to your book, please visit www.PacktPub.com.

Did you know that Packt offers eBook versions of every book published, with PDF and ePub files available? You can upgrade to the eBook version at www.PacktPub.com and as a print book customer, you are entitled to a discount on the eBook copy. Get in touch with us at service@packtpub.com for more details.

At www.PacktPub.com, you can also read a collection of free technical articles, sign up for a range of free newsletters and receive exclusive discounts and offers on Packt books and eBooks.

https://www2.packtpub.com/books/subscription/packtlib

Do you need instant solutions to your IT questions? PacktLib is Packt's online digital book library. Here, you can search, access, and read Packt's entire library of books.

Why subscribe?

- Fully searchable across every book published by Packt
- Copy and paste, print, and bookmark content
- On demand and accessible via a web browser

Free access for Packt account holders

If you have an account with Packt at www.PacktPub.com, you can use this to access PacktLib today and view 9 entirely free books. Simply use your login credentials for immediate access.

This book is dedicated to my angel, my inspiration, and my light — my son, Miguel — who never fails to amaze me in his endeavors to become a fine young man or cheer up the family.

Table of Contents

Preface

One can hardly develop new applications in our "now world" without duct-taping a lot of technologies together, be it new trend databases, messaging systems, or languages of all kinds. When talking about web development, things might get slightly more complicated as not only do you have to mix a lot of technologies together, but they must also work well with the applications accessing them (also known as web browsers). They should also be compatible with your deployment server, which is another story in itself!

In the Python world, where people deliver amazing desktop software following great guidelines such as the Zen of Python and PEP8, we have, at our disposal, a wide range of libraries and frameworks for creating great web applications, each with its own philosophy. Django, for example, is a bundle solution; it makes choices for you on how your project should look, what should it have, and how things should be done. Web2py is another framework solution that goes beyond and bundles even the IDE with it. These are great concepts, but if you want to create something simple, I would suggest you to do it somewhere else. They're usually good choices, but sometimes they're just too much (the latest Django version seems decisive in changing that; let's keep an eye on further developments).

Flask positions itself, not as a full-power out-of-the-box solution like both Django and Web2py, but as a minimalistic solution where you're given the bare minimum to work with and choose all the other stuff. That's very helpful when you want granular control of your application, when you want to precisely pick your components, or when your solution is simple (not simplistic, okay?).

This book is a response to that scenario of beautiful code and many options in the Web world. It tries to walk through the main concerns regarding web development, from security to content delivery and from session management to REST services and CRUD. Important modern concepts such as overengineering, quality and the development process are covered, so as to achieve better results from day one. To make the learning process smooth, subjects are presented without rush and followed by commented examples. The book also sets out to give readers real-world advice on how to prevent common problems with code.

Come learn how to create great Flask applications, delivering value to your projects and customers!

What this book covers

Chapter 1, *Flask in a Flask, I Mean, Book*, introduces you to Flask, explaining what it is, what it is not, and how it positions itself in the web framework world.

Chapter 2, *First App, How Hard Could it Be?*, covers the very first step toward Flask development, including environment setup, your very own "Hello World" app, and how templates enter into this equation. A fluffy chapter it is!

Chapter 3, *Man, Do I Like Templates!*, deals with face tags and filters progresses through the Jinja2 template engine and how it integrates with Flask. Things start to get a little serious from here!

Chapter 4, *Please Fill in This Form, Madam*, discusses how to handle forms (as forms are a fact in the web development life) with all the care they need using WTForms in all its glory!

Chapter 5, *Where Do You Store Your Stuff?*, introduces you to the concepts of relational and non-relational databases, covering how to handle both cases, and also when to.

Chapter 6, *But I Wanna REST Mom, Now!*, is a chapter on creating REST services (as the REST hype must be satisfied), manually and using the amazing Flask-Restless.

Chapter 7, *If Ain't Tested, It Ain't Game, Bro!*, is our quality-centric chapter where you learn to deliver quality through proper testing, the TDD and BDD way!

Chapter 8, *Tips and Tricks or Flask Wizardry 101*, is a dense chapter covering good practices, architecture, blueprints, debugging, and session management.

Chapter 9, Extensions, How I Love Thee, covers all those great Flask extensions not covered so far that will help you achieve the productivity the real world requires from you.

Chapter 10, What Now?, ends our development trip covering all the basics for a healthy deployment, and points you toward your next steps in the Flask world.

What you need for this book

To make the most of your reading experience, the reader is expected to have a machine with Ubuntu 14.x or superior installed as the examples are designed for this setup, a basic knowledge of Python (if you don't have this, refer to `http://learnxinyminutes.com/docs/python/` first), and a text editor with highlights of your likings (LightTable, Sublime, Atom). Other required software will be discussed through the chapters.

Who this book is for

This book targets Python developers, with some or no experience with web development, who wish to create minimalistic web applications. It is focused on those who want to become web developers as all the basics are covered to some extent, and also on those who already are familiar with web development using other frameworks, be it Python-based frameworks such as Django, Bottle, or Pyramid, or frameworks from other languages.

It is also important that you have a basic understanding of web technologies used to construct web pages, as is the case for CSS, JavaScript, and HTML. If that is not your background, please check out the W3Schools website (`http://w3schools.com/`) as it covers the basics of using these technologies. Also, if you're skilled with the Linux terminal, your life will be much easier throughout the whole book; try the link `https://help.ubuntu.com/community/UsingTheTerminal` if this is not the case.

Nonetheless, be assured that, if you have a basic knowledge of Python, you're more than capable of understanding the examples and the chapters; at the end of the book, you will be creating amazing web applications that perform well and are easy to maintain.

Conventions

In this book, you will find a number of styles of text that distinguish between different kinds of information. Here are some examples of these styles, and an explanation of their meaning.

Code words in text, database table names, folder names, filenames, file extensions, pathnames, dummy URLs, user input, and Twitter handles are shown as follows: "Enter the new project folder and create the `main.py` file".

A block of code is set as follows:

```
# coding:utf-8
from flask import Flask
app = Flask(__name__)

@app.route("/")
def hello():
    return "Hello World!"

if __name__ == "__main__":
    app.run()
```

Any command-line input or output is written as follows:

```
sudo pip install virtualenvwrapper
```

New terms and **important words** are shown in bold. Words that you see on the screen, in menus or dialog boxes for example, appear in the text like this: "Have you ever imagined what happens when you fill in a form on a website and click on that fancy **Send** button at the end of it?".

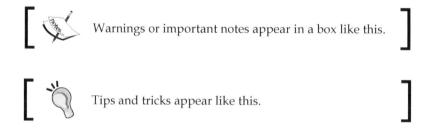

Warnings or important notes appear in a box like this.

Tips and tricks appear like this.

Reader feedback

Feedback from our readers is always welcome. Let us know what you think about this book—what you liked or may have disliked. Reader feedback is important for us to develop titles that you really get the most out of.

To send us general feedback, simply send an e-mail to feedback@packtpub.com, and mention the book title via the subject of your message.

If there is a topic that you have expertise in and you are interested in either writing or contributing to a book, see our author guide on www.packtpub.com/authors.

Customer support

Now that you are the proud owner of a Packt book, we have a number of things to help you to get the most from your purchase.

Downloading the example code

You can download the example code files for all Packt books you have purchased from your account at http://www.packtpub.com. If you purchased this book elsewhere, you can visit http://www.packtpub.com/support and register to have the files e-mailed directly to you.

Errata

Although we have taken every care to ensure the accuracy of our content, mistakes do happen. If you find a mistake in one of our books—maybe a mistake in the text or the code—we would be grateful if you would report this to us. By doing so, you can save other readers from frustration and help us improve subsequent versions of this book. If you find any errata, please report them by visiting http://www.packtpub.com/submit-errata, selecting your book, clicking on the **errata submission form** link, and entering the details of your errata. Once your errata are verified, your submission will be accepted and the errata will be uploaded on our website, or added to any list of existing errata, under the Errata section of that title. Any existing errata can be viewed by selecting your title from http://www.packtpub.com/support.

Piracy

Piracy of copyright material on the Internet is an ongoing problem across all media. At Packt, we take the protection of our copyright and licenses very seriously. If you come across any illegal copies of our works, in any form, on the Internet, please provide us with the location address or website name immediately so that we can pursue a remedy.

Please contact us at copyright@packtpub.com with a link to the suspected pirated material.

We appreciate your help in protecting our authors, and our ability to bring you valuable content.

Questions

You can contact us at questions@packtpub.com if you are having a problem with any aspect of the book, and we will do our best to address it.

1
Flask in a Flask,
I Mean, Book

What is Flask? It's a question that humanity has been pondering for millennia... well, actually, since 2010, when Armin Ronacher first committed to the project. Flask is a Web framework and is quite different from what most people are used to working with. It is less presumptuous about how your application should look or what you should use to make it available. The BSD licensed package has all this!

An introduction to Flask and its features

The Flask framework is actually a glue, a very nice one, that sticks together the amazing Werkzeug and Jinja2 frameworks, responsible for answering requests and presenting the output (HTML, maybe). In the MVC architecture, also known as Model-View-Controller, Flask covers C and V. But where is M? Flask does not provide you with an integrated model layer out-of-the-box as that is not actually needed for a web application. If you do need to work with a database, just pick your database solution from the many available and create your own model layer, which is not hard, and be happy! The concept of a micro-framework, with good intentions and made just for Flask, is all about giving you the the smallest (but also the most useful) feature set you need, and one that won't get in the way.

Just what are the features that must be in the framework?

- A development server and debugger (sanity-friendly)
- Unicode support (Latin language-friendly)
- WSGI compliance (uWsgi-friendly)
- A unit-test client client (code with quality)
- URL routing (it brings tears to my eyes, it's so beautiful!)

- Request dispatching
- Secure cookies
- Sessions
- Jinja2 templates (tags, filters, macros, and more)

With that much, you can handle Ajax requests, browser requests, and user sessions between requests; route HTTP requests to your controllers; evaluate form data; respond to HTML and JSON; and so on.

That is nice, but is Flask not an MVC framework? Well, that's arguable. If a web framework does not implement an MVC antipattern, such as handling requests in the view or mixing models and controllers, it could potentially facilitate an MVC, which, in my opinion, is as good as it gets because it does not enforce your application structure.

 Flask is not an MVC framework as it does not implement the model layer, although it does not restrict you in any way if you wish to create your own.

If you need a simple, single-file web application that receives a form and gives back an answer, HTML or not, Flask will help you with that, easily. If you need a multilayer, high-depth modularized Facebook clone, Flask can also be there for you.

So, what did we learn so far?

- Flask was born in 2010
- Flask is a minimalistic web framework based on Jinja2 and Werkzeug
- Flask does not enforce a specific project architecture

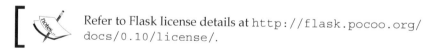 Refer to Flask license details at http://flask.pocoo.org/docs/0.10/license/.

Right now, you might be wondering which of your neat project ideas could be done with Flask. That's the spirit! What about thinking together on this one?

Flask does not come with bundled functionality in terms of database integration, a forms library, administration interface, or migration tools. You can have these through extensions, which will be discussed soon enough, but they are all external to Flask. If you need these extensions right at the beginning of your project and you don't want to set it up (or can't spare the time to), you might do better with a full-fledged MVC all-in one, low-cohesive, and high-coupling framework such as Django.

Now, imagine you need to build a website with a single form, such as a `http://cashcash.cc/` clone, which receives a form and returns the current currency trade values; Flask could help conclude your project really fast.

Let's think further. What if you need a specific set of libraries to work together in your project and you don't want the web framework getting in the way; that's another very good scenario for Flask as it gives you the bare minimum and lets you put together everything else you may need. Some frameworks have such a high level of coupling (read **dependency**) on their own components that you may have a serious problem if you want to use a specific alternative.

For example, you may want to use a NoSQL database in your project; however, if you do so, some components of your project may stop working (for example: an administrative component).

Basically, if you have the time to spare, if you're doing something simple, if you want to implement your own architecture solution, or if you need granular control of the components used in your project, Flask is the web framework for you.

Summary

Now, let's talk about awesomeness, your awesomeness after reading this book—you will be capable of handling HTTP and Ajax requests; creating fully featured web applications with database integration (SQL and NoSQL) and REST services; using Flask extensions (forms, caching, logging, debugging, auth, permissions, and so on); and modularizing and unit- and feature-testing your applications.

I hope you enjoy this book and build great things with what you learn here

2

First App, How Hard Could it Be?

After a full chapter without a single line of code, you need this, right? In this chapter, we will write our first app explained line by line; we will also cover how to set up our environment, what tools to use for development, and how to work with HTML in our app.

Hello World

The first app one writes when learning a new technology is usually a Hello World app, which consists of the minimum possible code necessary to start a simple application and show the text "Hello World!". Let's do exactly that using Flask.

This book is optimized for **Python 2.x**, so, that's the version I advise you to use from now on. All the examples and code are aimed at that Python version, which is the default in most Linux distributions.

Prerequisites and tools

First, let's make sure our environment is properly configured. For this course, I assume you are using a Debian-like Linux distribution, such as Mint (http://www.linuxmint.com/) or Ubuntu (http://ubuntu.com/). All the instructions will be geared towards these systems.

Let's begin by installing the required Debian packages with apt-get as follows:

```
sudo apt-get install python-dev python-pip
```

This will install the Python development tools and libraries required for compiling Python packages, and pip: a neat tool you can use to install Python packages from the command line. On with it! Let's install our virtual environment managing tool:

```
sudo pip install virtualenvwrapper
echo "source /usr/local/bin/virtualenvwrapper.sh" >> ~/.bashrc
```

To explain what we just did: `sudo` tells our OS that we want administrative privileges to run the next command, and `pip` is the default Python package management tool and helps us install the `virtualenvwrapper` package. The second command statement adds a command to load the `virtualenvwrapper.sh` script together with the console, so that commands work inside your shell (we'll be using it, by the way).

Setting up a virtual environment

A virtual environment is the way Python isolates full package environments from one another. This means you can easily manage dependencies. Imagine you want to define the minimum necessary packages for a project; a virtual environment would be perfect to let you test and export the list of needed packages. We will discuss it later on. Now, create a new terminal pressing *Ctrl + Shift + T* on your keyboard and create our *hello world* environment like this:

```
mkvirtualenv hello
pip install flask
```

The first line creates our environment with the name "hello". You will also *automatically* load that environment into the current terminal. You can deactivate your virtual environment by typing `deactivate` and you can load it again with the following command:

```
workon hello  # substitute hello with the desired environment name if
needed
```

The second line tells pip to install the Flask package in the current virtual environment, `hello` in this case.

Understanding the "Hello World" app

Given the environment set, what should we use to write our beautiful code? An editor or an IDE? If you're working on a low budget, try Light Table editor (`http://lighttable.com/`). Free, fast, and easy to use (*Ctrl + Spacebar* gives you access to all available options), it also has workspace support! Can't get any better for the money. If you're a lucky one with $200 to spare (or if you have a free license `https://www.jetbrains.com/pycharm/buy/`), just fork out for the PyCharm IDE which is pretty much the best IDE for Python Web development. Now let's move on.

Create a folder that will hold your project files (you don't need to but people will like you more if you do), as follows:

```
mkdir hello_world
```

Enter the new project folder and create the `main.py` file:

```
cd hello_world
touch main.py
```

The `main.py` file will have the whole "Hello World" application in it. Our `main.py` content should be like this:

```
# coding:utf-8
from flask import Flask
app = Flask(__name__)


@app.route("/")
def hello():
    return "Hello World!"


if __name__ == "__main__":
    app.run()
```

Downloading the example code

You can download the example code files for all Packt books you have purchased from your account at `http://www.packtpub.com`. If you purchased this book elsewhere, you can visit `http://www.packtpub.com/support` and register to have the files e-mailed directly to you.

Wow! That took some typing, right? No? Yeah, I know. So, what did we just do?

The first line states that our `main.py` file should use `utf-8` encoding. All the cool kids do that so don't be mean to your non-English pals and use that in all your Python files (doing so might help you avoid some nasty bugs in big projects).

In the second and third lines we import our Flask class and instantiate it. The name of our application is "app". Pretty much everything is related to it: views, blueprints, config, and so on. The argument, `__name__` is required and is used to tell the application where to look for resources such as static content or templates.

In order to create our "Hello World", we need to tell our Flask instance how to respond when a user tries to access our Web application (using a browser or whatever). For that purpose, Flask has routes.

Routes are the way Flask reads a request header and decides which view should respond to that request. It does so by analyzing the path part of the requested URL and finding which route is registered with that path.

In the *hello world* example, in line 5, we use the route decorator to register the `hello` function to the path `"/"`. Every time an app receives a request in which the path is `"/"`, `hello` will respond to that request. The following snippet shows how to check the path part of a URL:

```
from urlparse import urlparse
parsed = urlparse("https://www.google.com/")
assert parsed.path == "/"
```

You could also have multiple routes mapped to the same function, like so:

```
@app.route("/")
@app.route("/index")
def hello():
    return "Hello World!"
```

In this case, both the `"/"` and `"/index"` paths would map to `hello`.

In lines 6 and 7 we have the function that will respond the request. Notice that it receives no parameters and responds –with a familiar string. It receives no parameters because the request data, like a submitted form, is accessed through a thread-safe variable called **request** that we will see more about in upcoming chapters.

With regard to the response, Flask can respond to requests in numerous formats. In our example, we respond with a plain string, but we could also respond with a JSON or HTML string.

Lines 9 and 10 are simple. They check whether `main.py` is being called as a script or as a module. If it is as a script, it will run the built-in development server that comes bundled with Flask. Let's try that:

python main.py

Your terminal console will output something like this:

Running on http://127.0.0.1:5000/ (Press CTRL+C to quit)

Just open `http://127.0.0.1:5000/` in your browser to see your app working.

Running `main.py` as a script is usually a very simple and handy setup. Usually, you have Flask-Script to handle calling the development server for you and other setups.

If you used `main.py` as a module, just import it as follows:

```
from main import what_I_want
```

You would usually do something like this to import an app factory function in your testing code.

That's pretty much all there is to know about our "*Hello World*" application. One thing our world application lacks is a fun factor. So let's add that; let's make your application fun! Maybe some HTML, CSS, and JavaScript could do the trick here. Let's try that!

Serving HTML pages

First, to make our `hello` function respond with HTML, all we have to do is change it like this:

```
def hello():
    return "<html><head><title>Hi there!</title></head><body>Hello
World!</body></html>", 200
```

In the preceding example, `hello` is returning a HTML formatted string and a number. The string will be parsed as HTML by default while `200` is an optional HTTP code indicating a successful response. `200` is returned by default.

If you refresh your browser with *F5*, you'll notice that nothing has changed. That's why the Flask development server is not reloading when the source changes. That only happens when you run your application in debug mode. So let's do that:

```
app = Flask(__name__)
app.debug=True
```

Now go to the terminal where your application is running, type `Ctrl + C` then restart the server. You will notice a new output besides the URL where your server is running — something about "stat". That indicates your server will reload the code on source modification. That's nice, but did you spot the crime we just committed: defining our template inside the function that handles the response? Be careful, the MVC gods might be watching. Let's separate where we define our view from where we define our controller. Create a folder called templates and a file called `index.html` inside it. The `index.html` file content should be like this:

```
<html>
<head><title>Hi there!</title></head>
<body>Hello World!</body>
</html>
```

Now change your code like this:

```
from flask import Flask, render_response
@app.route("/")
def hello():
    return render_template("index.html")
```

Did you see what we did there? `render_response` is capable of loading templates from the `templates/` folder (a default for Flask) and you can render it just by returning the output.

Now let's add some JavaScript and CSS styles. By default, the Flask built-in development server serves all files in your `project` folder that are in a subfolder called `static`. Let's create ours and add some files to it. Your project tree should look like this:

```
project/
-main.py
-templates/
--index.html
-static/
--js
---jquery.min.js
---foundation.min.js
---modernizr.js
--css
---styles.css
---foundation.min.css
```

Notice that I add files from the `foundation.zurb` framework, a nice CSS framework available in `http://foundation.zurb.com/`. I advise you to do the same in order to have a modern, good-looking site. The path to the static files in your template should look like this:

```
<script src='/static/js/modernizr.js'></script>
```

The folder, `/static` before the real file path is a route served by default by Flask that only works in debug mode. In production, you would have the HTTP server serving your static files for you. See the attached code for this chapter for the full example.

Try improving the *hello world* example with some nice CSS styling!

Summary

Setting up a development environment is a very important task, and we just did this! Creating a "*Hello World*" application is a great way to introduce a new technology to someone. We also did that. At last, we learned how to serve an HTML page and static files, which is pretty much what most Web applications do. You acquired all these skills in this chapter, and I hope the process has been quite easy but fulfilling!

In the next chapter, we add a little sauce to our challenges by getting more adventurous with templates. We'll learn how to use Jinja2 components to create powerful templates that allow us to do more with less typing. See you there!

3
Man, Do I Like Templates!

As stated previously, Flask gives you the VC of MVC out-of-the-box. In this chapter, we will discuss what Jinja2 is, and how Flask uses Jinja2 to implement the View layer and awe you. Be prepared!

What is Jinja2 and how is it coupled with Flask?

Jinja2 is a library found at http://jinja.pocoo.org/; you can use it to produce formatted text with bundled logic. Unlike the Python format function, which only allows you to replace markup with variable content, you can have a control structure, such as a for loop, inside a template string and use Jinja2 to parse it. Let's consider this example:

```
from jinja2 import Template
x = """
<p>Uncle Scrooge nephews</p>
<ul>
{% for i in my_list %}
<li>{{ i }}</li>
{% endfor %}
</ul>
"""
template = Template(x)
# output is an unicode string
print template.render(my_list=['Huey', 'Dewey', 'Louie'])
```

In the preceding code, we have a very simple example where we create a template string with a for loop control structure ("for tag", for short) that iterates over a list variable called my_list and prints the element inside a "li HTML tag" using curly braces {{ }} notation.

Notice that you could call `render` in the template instance as many times as needed with different key-value arguments, also called the template context. A context variable may have any valid Python variable name — that is, anything in the format given by the regular expression *[a-zA-Z_][a-zA-Z0-9_]*.*

For a full overview on regular expressions (**Regex** for short) with Python, visit `https://docs.python.org/2/library/re.html`. Also, take a look at this nice online tool for Regex testing `http://pythex.org/`.

A more elaborate example would make use of an environment class instance, which is a central, configurable, extensible class that may be used to load templates in a more organized way.

Do you follow where we are going here? This is the basic principle behind Jinja2 and Flask: it prepares an environment for you, with a few responsive defaults, and gets your wheels in motion.

What can you do with Jinja2?

Jinja2 is pretty slick. You can use it with template files or strings; you can use it to create formatted text, such as HTML, XML, Markdown, and e-mail content; you can put together templates, reuse templates, and extend templates; you can even use extensions with it. The possibilities are countless, and combined with nice debugging features, auto-escaping, and full unicode support.

Auto-escaping is a Jinja2 configuration where everything you print in a template is interpreted as plain text, if not explicitly requested otherwise. Imagine a variable *x* has its value set to `<b>b</b>`. If auto-escaping is enabled, `{{ x }}` in a template would print the string as given. If auto-escaping is off, which is the Jinja2 default (Flask's default is on), the resulting text would be b.

Let's understand a few concepts before covering how Jinja2 allows us to do our coding.

First, we have the previously mentioned curly braces. Double curly braces are a delimiter that allows you to evaluate a variable or function from the provided context and print it into the template:

```
from jinja2 import Template
# create the template
t = Template("{{ variable }}")
```

```
# - Built-in Types -
t.render(variable='hello you')
>> u"hello you"
t.render(variable=100)
>> u"100"
# you can evaluate custom classes instances
class A(object):
  def __str__(self):
    return "__str__"
  def __unicode__(self):
    return u"__unicode__"
  def __repr__(self):
    return u"__repr__"
# - Custom Objects Evaluation -
# __unicode__ has the highest precedence in evaluation
# followed by __str__ and __repr__
t.render(variable=A())
>> u"__unicode__"
```

In the preceding example, we see how to use curly braces to evaluate variables in your template. First, we evaluate a string and then an integer. Both result in a unicode string. If we evaluate a class of our own, we must make sure there is a __unicode__ method defined, as it is called during the evaluation. If a __unicode__ method is not defined, the evaluation falls back to __str__ and __repr__, sequentially. This is easy. Furthermore, what if we want to evaluate a function? Well, just call it:

```
from jinja2 import Template
# create the template
t = Template("{{ fnc() }}")
t.render(fnc=lambda: 10)
>> u"10"
# evaluating a function with argument
t = Template("{{ fnc(x) }}")
t.render(fnc=lambda v: v, x='20')
>> u"20"
t = Template("{{ fnc(v=30) }}")
t.render(fnc=lambda v: v)
>> u"30"
```

To output the result of a function in a template, just call the function as any regular Python function. The function return value will be evaluated normally. If you're familiar with Django, you might notice a slight difference here. In Django, you do not need the parentheses to call a function, or even pass arguments to it. In Flask, the parentheses are *always* needed if you want the function return evaluated.

The following two examples show the difference between Jinja2 and Django function call in a template:

```
{# flask syntax #}
{{ some_function() }}

{# django syntax #}
{{ some_function }}
```

You can also evaluate Python math operations. Take a look:

```
from jinja2 import Template
# no context provided / needed
Template("{{ 3 + 3 }}").render()
>> u"6"
Template("{{ 3 - 3 }}").render()
>> u"0"
Template("{{ 3 * 3 }}").render()
>> u"9"
Template("{{ 3 / 3 }}").render()
>> u"1"
```

Other math operators will also work. You may use the curly braces delimiter to access and evaluate lists and dictionaries:

```
from jinja2 import Template
Template("{{ my_list[0] }}").render(my_list=[1, 2, 3])
>> u'1'
Template("{{ my_list['foo'] }}").render(my_list={'foo': 'bar'})
>> u'bar'
# and here's some magic
Template("{{ my_list.foo }}").render(my_list={'foo': 'bar'})
>> u'bar'
```

To access a list or dictionary value, just use normal plain Python notation. With dictionaries, you can also access a key value using variable access notation, which is pretty neat.

Besides the curly braces delimiter, Jinja2 also has the curly braces/percentage delimiter, which uses the notation `{% stmt %}` and is used to execute statements, which may be a control statement or not. Its usage depends on the statement, where control statements have the following notation:

```
{% stmt %}
{% endstmt %}
```

The first tag has the statement name, while the second is the closing tag, which has the name of the statement appended with `end` in the beginning. You must be aware that a non-control statement *may* not have a closing tag. Let's look at some examples:

```
{% block content %}
{% for i in items %}
{{ i }} - {{ i.price }}
{% endfor %}
{% endblock %}
```

The preceding example is a little more complex than what we have been seeing. It uses a control statement `for` loop inside a block statement (you can have a statement inside another), which is not a control statement, as it does not control execution flow in the template. Inside the `for` loop you see that the `i` variable is being printed together with the associated price (defined elsewhere).

A last delimiter you should know is `{# comments go here #}`. It is a multi-line delimiter used to declare comments. Let's see two examples that have the same result:

```
{# first example #}
{#
second example
#}
```

Both comment delimiters hide the content between `{#` and `#}`. As can been seen, this delimiter works for one-line comments and multi-line comments, what makes it very convenient.

Control structures

We have a nice set of built-in control structures defined by default in Jinja2. Let's begin our studies on it with the `if` statement.

```
{% if true %}Too easy{% endif %}
{% if true == true == True %}True and true are the same{% endif %}
{% if false == false == False %}False and false also are the same{%
endif %}
{% if none == none == None %}There's also a lowercase None{% endif %}
{% if 1 >= 1 %}Compare objects like in plain python{% endif %}
{% if 1 == 2 %}This won't be printed{% else %}This will{% endif %}
{% if "apples" != "oranges" %}All comparison operators work = ]{%
endif %}
{% if something %}elif is also supported{% elif something_else %}^_^{%
endif %}
```

The `if` control statement is beautiful! It behaves just like a `python` `if` statement. As seen in the preceding code, you can use it to compare objects in a very easy fashion. "else" and "elif" are also fully supported.

You may also have noticed that `true` and `false`, non-capitalized, were used together with plain Python Booleans, `True` and `False`. As a design decision to avoid confusion, all Jinja2 templates have a lowercase alias for `True`, `False`, and `None`. By the way, lowercase syntax is the preferred way to go.

If needed, and you should avoid this scenario, you may group comparisons together in order to change precedence evaluation. See the following example:

```
{% if  5 < 10 < 15 %}true{%else%}false{% endif %}
{% if  (5 < 10) < 15 %}true{%else%}false{% endif %}
{% if  5 < (10 < 15) %}true{%else%}false{% endif %}
```

The expected output for the preceding example is `true`, `true`, and `false`. The first two lines are pretty straightforward. In the third line, first, `(10<15)` is evaluated to `True`, which is a subclass of `int`, where `True == 1`. Then `5 < True` is evaluated, which is certainly false.

The `for` statement is pretty important. One can hardly think of a serious Web application that does not have to show a list of some kind at some point. The `for` statement can iterate over any iterable instance and has a very simple, Python-like syntax:

```
{% for item in my_list %}
{{ item }}{# print evaluate item #}
{% endfor %}
{# or #}
{% for key, value in my_dictionary.items() %}
{{ key }}: {{ value }}
{% endfor %}
```

In the first statement, we have the opening tag indicating that we will iterate over `my_list` items and each item will be referenced by the name `item`. The name `item` will be available inside the `for` loop context only.

In the second statement, we have an iteration over the key value tuples that form `my_dictionary`, which should be a dictionary (if the variable name wasn't suggestive enough). Pretty simple, right? The `for` loop also has a few tricks in store for you.

When building HTML lists, it's a common requirement to mark each list item in alternating colors in order to improve readability or mark the first or/and last item with some special markup. Those behaviors can be achieved in a Jinja2 for-loop through access to a loop variable available inside the block context. Let's see some examples:

```
{% for i in ['a', 'b', 'c', 'd'] %}
{% if loop.first %}This is the first iteration{% endif %}
{% if loop.last %}This is the last iteration{% endif %}
{{ loop.cycle('red', 'blue') }}{# print red or blue alternating #}
{{ loop.index }} - {{ loop.index0 }} {# 1 indexed index - 0 indexed
index #}
{# reverse 1 indexed index - reverse 0 indexed index #}
{{ loop.revindex }} - {{ loop.revindex0 }}
{% endfor %}
```

The `for` loop statement, as in Python, also allow the use of `else`, but with a slightly different meaning. In Python, when you use `else` with `for`, the `else` block is only executed if it was *not* reached through a `break` command like this:

```
for i in [1, 2, 3]:
  pass
else:
  print "this will be printed"
for i in [1, 2, 3]:
  if i == 3:
    break
else:
  print "this will never not be printed"
```

As seen in the preceding code snippet, the `else` block will only be executed in a `for` loop if the execution was never broken by a `break` command. With Jinja2, the `else` block is executed when the `for` iterable is empty. For example:

```
{% for i in [] %}
{{ i }}
{% else %}I'll be printed{% endfor %}
{% for i in ['a'] %}
{{ i }}
{% else %}I won't{% endfor %}
```

As we are talking about loops and breaks, there are two important things to know: the Jinja2 `for` loop does not support `break` or `continue`. Instead, to achieve the expected behavior, you should use loop filtering as follows:

```
{% for i in [1, 2, 3, 4, 5] if i > 2 %}
value: {{ i }}; loop.index: {{ loop.index }}
{%- endfor %}
```

In the first tag you see a normal `for` loop together with an `if` condition. You should consider that condition as a real list filter, as the index itself is only counted per iteration. Run the preceding example and the output will be the following:

```
value:3; index: 1
value:4; index: 2
value:5; index: 3
```

Look at the last observation in the preceding example — in the second tag, do you see the dash in `{%-`? It tells the renderer that there should be no empty new lines before the tag at each iteration. Try our previous example without the dash and compare the results to see what changes.

We'll now look at three very important statements used to build templates from different files: `block`, `extends`, and `include`.

`block` and `extends` always work together. The first is used to define "overwritable" blocks in a template, while the second defines a parent template that has blocks, for the current template. Let's see an example:

```
# coding:utf-8
with open('parent.txt', 'w') as file:
    file.write("""
{% block template %}parent.txt{% endblock %}
===========
I am a powerful psychic and will tell you your past

{#- "past" is the block identifier #}
{% block past %}
You had pimples by the age of 12.
{%- endblock %}

Tremble before my power!!!""".strip())

with open('child.txt', 'w') as file:
    file.write("""
{% extends "parent.txt" %}

{# overwriting the block called template from parent.txt #}
{% block template %}child.txt{% endblock %}

{#- overwriting the block called past from parent.txt #}
{% block past %}
You've bought an ebook recently.
{%- endblock %}""".strip())
with open('other.txt', 'w') as file:
    file.write("""
```

```
{% extends "child.txt" %}
{% block template %}other.txt{% endblock %}""".strip())

from jinja2 import Environment, FileSystemLoader

env = Environment()
# tell the environment how to load templates
env.loader = FileSystemLoader('.')
# look up our template
tmpl = env.get_template('parent.txt')
# render it to default output
print tmpl.render()
print ""
# loads child.html and its parent
tmpl = env.get_template('child.txt')
print tmpl.render()
# loads other.html and its parent
env.get_template('other.txt').render()
```

Do you see the inheritance happening, between child.txt and parent.txt? parent.txt is a simple template with two block statements, called template and past. When you render parent.txt directly, its blocks are printed "as is", because they were not overwritten. In child.txt, we extend the parent.txt template and overwrite all its blocks. By doing that, we can have different information in specific parts of a template without having to rewrite the whole thing.

With other.txt, for example, we extend the child.txt template and overwrite only the block-named template. You can overwrite blocks from a direct parent template or from any of its parents.

If you were defining an index.txt page, you could have default blocks in it that would be overwritten when needed, saving lots of typing.

Explaining the last example, Python-wise, is pretty simple. First, we create a Jinja2 environment (we talked about this earlier) and tell it how to load our templates, then we load the desired template directly. We do not have to bother telling the environment how to find parent templates, nor do we need to preload them.

The include statement is probably the easiest statement so far. It allows you to render a template inside another in a very easy fashion. Let's look at an example:

```
with open('base.txt', 'w') as file:
  file.write("""
{{ myvar }}
You wanna hear a dirty joke?
{% include 'joke.txt' %}
```

```
""".strip())
with open('joke.txt', 'w') as file:
    file.write("""
A boy fell in a mud puddle. {{ myvar }}
""".strip())

from jinja2 import Environment, FileSystemLoader

env = Environment()
# tell the environment how to load templates
env.loader = FileSystemLoader('.')
print env.get_template('base.txt').render(myvar='Ha ha!')
```

In the preceding example, we render the `joke.txt` template inside `base.txt`. As `joke.txt` is rendered inside `base.txt`, it also has full access to the `base.txt` context, so `myvar` is printed normally.

Finally, we have the `set` statement. It allows you to define variables for inside the template context. Its use is pretty simple:

```
{% set x = 10 %}
{{ x }}
{% set x, y, z = 10, 5+5, "home" %}
{{ x }} - {{ y }} - {{ z }}
```

In the preceding example, if x was given by a complex calculation or a database query, it would make much more sense to have it *cached* in a variable, if it is to be reused across the template. As seen in the example, you can also assign a value to multiple variables at once.

Macros

Macros are the closest to coding you'll get inside Jinja2 templates. The macro definition and usage are similar to plain Python functions, so it is pretty easy. Let's try an example:

```
with open('formfield.html', 'w') as file:
    file.write('''
{% macro input(name, value='', label='') %}
{% if label %}
<label for='{{ name }}'>{{ label }}</label>
{% endif %}
<input id='{{ name }}' name='{{ name }}' value='{{ value }}'></input>
{% endmacro %}'''.strip())
with open('index.html', 'w') as file:
```

```
   file.write('''
{% from 'formfield.html' import input %}
<form method='get' action='.'>
{{ input('name', label='Name:') }}
<input type='submit' value='Send'></input>
</form>
'''.strip())

from jinja2 import Environment, FileSystemLoader

env = Environment()
env.loader = FileSystemLoader('.')
print env.get_template('index.html').render()
```

In the preceding example, we create a macro that accepts a `name` argument and two optional arguments: `value` and `label`. Inside the `macro` block, we define what should be output. Notice we can use other statements inside a macro, just like a template. In `index.html` we import the input macro from inside `formfield.html`, as if `formfield` was a module and input was a Python function using the `import` statement. If needed, we could even rename our input macro like this:

```
{% from 'formfield.html' import input as field_input %}
```

You can also import `formfield` as a module and use it as follows:

```
{% import 'formfield.html' as formfield %}
```

When using macros, there is a special case where you want to allow any named argument to be passed into the macro, as you would in a Python function (for example, `**kwargs`). With Jinja2 macros, these values are, by default, available in a `kwargs` dictionary that does not need to be explicitly defined in the macro signature. For example:

```
# coding:utf-8
with open('formfield.html', 'w') as file:
    file.write('''
{% macro input(name) -%}
<input id='{{ name }}' name='{{ name }}' {% for k,v in kwargs.items()
-%}{{ k }}='{{ v }}' {% endfor %}></input>
{%- endmacro %}
'''.strip())with open('index.html', 'w') as file:
    file.write('''
{% from 'formfield.html' import input %}
{# use method='post' whenever sending sensitive data over HTTP #}
<form method='post' action='.'>
{{ input('name', type='text') }}
```

```
{{ input('passwd', type='password') }}
<input type='submit' value='Send'></input>
</form>
'''.strip())

from jinja2 import Environment, FileSystemLoader

env = Environment()
env.loader = FileSystemLoader('.')
print env.get_template('index.html').render()
```

As you can see, `kwargs` is available even though you did not define a `kwargs` argument in the macro signature.

Macros have a few clear advantages over plain templates, that you notice with the `include` statement:

- You do not have to worry about variable names in the template using macros
- You can define the exact required context for a macro block through the macro signature
- You can define a macro library inside a template and import only what is needed

Commonly used macros in a Web application include a macro to render pagination, another to render fields, and another to render forms. You could have others, but these are pretty common use cases.

 Regarding our previous example, it is good practice to use HTTPS (also known as, Secure HTTP) to send sensitive information, such as passwords, over the Internet. Be careful about that!

Extensions

Extensions are the way Jinja2 allows you to extend its vocabulary. Extensions are not enabled by default, so you can enable an extension only when and if you need, and start using it without much trouble:

```
env = Environment(extensions=['jinja2.ext.do',
    'jinja2.ext.with_'])
```

In the preceding code, we have an example where you create an environment with two extensions enabled: `do` and `with`. Those are the extensions we will study in this chapter.

As the name suggests, the do extension allows you to "do stuff". Inside a do tag, you're allowed to execute Python expressions with full access to the template context. Flask-Empty, a popular Flask boilerplate available at https://github.com/italomaia/flask-empty uses the do extension to update a dictionary in one of its macros, for example. Let's see how we could do the same:

```
{% set x = {1:'home', '2':'boat'} %}
{% do x.update({3: 'bar'}) %}
{%- for key,value in x.items() %}
{{ key }} - {{ value }}
{%- endfor %}
```

In the preceding example, we create the x variable with a dictionary, then we update it with {3: 'bar'}. You don't usually need to use the do extension but, when you do, a lot of coding is saved.

The with extension is also very simple. You use it whenever you need to create block scoped variables. Imagine you have a value you need cached in a variable for a brief moment; this would be a good use case. Let's see an example:

```
{% with age = user.get_age() %}
My age: {{ age }}
{% endwith %}
My age: {{ age }}{# no value here #}
```

As seen in the example, age exists only inside the with block. Also, variables set inside a with block will only exist inside it. For example:

```
{% with %}
{% set count = query.count() %}
Current Stock: {{ count }}
Diff: {{ prev_count - count }}
{% endwith %}
{{ count }} {# empty value #}
```

Filters

Filters are a marvelous thing about Jinja2! This tool allows you to process a constant or variable before printing it to the template. The goal is to implement the formatting you want, strictly in the template.

To use a filter, just call it using the pipe operator like this:

```
{% set name = 'junior' %}
{{ name|capitalize }} {# output is Junior #}
```

Its name is passed to the **capitalize** filter that processes it and returns the capitalized value. To inform arguments to the filter, just call it like a function, like this:

```
{{ ['Adam', 'West']|join(' ') }} {# output is Adam West #}
```

The `join` filter will join all values from the passed iterable, putting the provided argument between them.

Jinja2 has an enormous quantity of available filters by default. That means we can't cover them all here, but we can certainly cover a few. `capitalize` and `lower` were seen already. Let's look at some further examples:

```
{# prints default value if input is undefined #}
{{ x|default('no opinion') }}
{# prints default value if input evaluates to false #}
{{ none|default('no opinion', true) }}
{# prints input as it was provided #}
{{ 'some opinion'|default('no opinion') }}

{# you can use a filter inside a control statement #}
{# sort by key case-insensitive #}
{% for key in {'A':3, 'b':2, 'C':1}|dictsort %}{{ key }}{% endfor %}
{# sort by key case-sensitive #}
{% for key in {'A':3, 'b':2, 'C':1}|dictsort(true) %}{{ key }}{%
endfor %}
{# sort by value #}
{% for key in {'A':3, 'b':2, 'C':1}|dictsort(false, 'value') %}{{ key
}}{% endfor %}
{{ [3, 2, 1]|first }} - {{ [3, 2, 1]|last }}
{{ [3, 2, 1]|length }} {# prints input length #}
{# same as in python #}
{{ '%s, =D'|format("I'm John") }}
{{ "He has two daughters"|replace('two', 'three') }}
{# safe prints the input without escaping it first#}
{{ '<input name="stuff" />'|safe }}
{{ "there are five words here"|wordcount }}
```

Try the preceding example to see exactly what each filter does.

After reading this much about Jinja2, you're probably thinking: "Jinja2 is cool but this is a book about Flask. Show me the Flask stuff!". Ok, ok, I can do that!

Of what we have seen so far, almost everything can be used with Flask with no modifications. As Flask manages the Jinja2 environment for you, you don't have to worry about creating file loaders and stuff like that. One thing you should be aware of, though, is that, because you don't instantiate the Jinja2 environment yourself, you can't really pass to the class constructor, the extensions you want to activate.

To activate an extension, add it to Flask during the application setup as follows:

```
from flask import Flask
app = Flask(__name__)
app.jinja_env.add_extension('jinja2.ext.do')  # or jinja2.ext.with_
if __name__ == '__main__':
  app.run()
```

Messing with the template context

As seen in *Chapter 2, First App, How Hard Could it Be?*, you can use the render_template method to load a template from the templates folder and then render it as a response.

```
from flask import Flask, render_template
app = Flask(__name__)


@app.route("/")
def hello():
    return render_template("index.html")
```

If you want to add values to the template context, as seen in some of the examples in this chapter, you would have to add non-positional arguments to render_template:

```
from flask import Flask, render_template
app = Flask(__name__)


@app.route("/")
def hello():
    return render_template("index.html", my_age=28)
```

In the preceding example, my_age would be available in the index.html context, where {{ my_age }} would be translated to 28. my_age could have virtually any value you want to exhibit, actually.

Now, what if you want *all* your views to have a specific value in their context, like a version value—some special code or function; how would you do it? Flask offers you the context_processor decorator to accomplish that. You just have to annotate a function that returns a dictionary and you're ready to go. For example:

```
from flask import Flask, render_response
app = Flask(__name__)

@app.context_processor
def luck_processor():
  from random import randint
  def lucky_number():
```

```
    return randint(1, 10)
  return dict(lucky_number=lucky_number)

@app.route("/")
def hello():
  # lucky_number will be available in the index.html context by
default
  return render_template("index.html")
```

Summary

In this chapter, we saw how to render templates using only Jinja2, how control statements look and how to use them, how to write a comment, how to print variables in a template, how to write and use macros, how to load and use extensions, and how to register context processors. I don't know about you, but this chapter felt like a lot of information! I strongly advise you to run the experiment with the examples. Knowing your way around Jinja2 will save you a lot of headaches.

Next chapter, we will be studying forms with Flask. Expect a lot of examples and complementary code, as forms are the doors you open from your Web application to the Web. Most problems arise from the Web, as well as most of your data.

4
Please Fill in This Form, Madam

Have you ever imagined what happens when you fill in a form on a website and click on that fancy **Send** button at the end of it? Well, all the data you wrote — comment, name, checkbox, or whatever — is encoded and sent through a protocol to the server, which then routes that information to the Web application. The Web application will validate the data origin, read the form, validate the data syntactically then semantically, and then decide what to do with it. Do you see that long chain of events where every link might be the cause of a problem? That's forms for you.

In any case, there is nothing to fear! Flask can help you in those steps but there are also tools specifically designed for this purpose. In this chapter, we will learn:

- How to write and handle forms with Flask
- How to validate form data
- How to use WTForms to validate forms with Flask
- How to implement cross-site request forgery protection

This will actually be a fairly smooth chapter, with lots of new info but nothing complex. Hope you enjoy it!

HTML forms for the faint of heart

HTML is, pretty much, the language in which the Web is written. With the help of special markups called **tags**, it's possible to add meaning and context to plain text, turning it into HTML. For us, HTML is a means to an end. So, if you want to learn more about it, please open `http://www.w3schools.com/html/` in your preferred browser. We are not covering HTML syntax fully, nor all the beautiful magic involved in the process.

Although we will not cover HTML extensively, we will cover HTML specifically; by this, I refer to the `<form>` tag. Here is the deal: every time you open a webpage and there are a few blank fields for you to fill in, you're most likely filling in an HTML form. That's the plainest way to transfer data from your browser to a server. How does that work? Let's see an example:

```
<!-- example 1 -->
<form method='post' action='.'>
<input type='text' name='username' />
<input type='password' name='passwd' />
<input type='submit' />
</form>
```

In the preceding example, we have a full login form. Its beginning is defined by the `<form>` tag, which has two non-required attributes: `method` and `action`. The `method` attribute defines how you want your form data to be sent to the server when it is sent. Its value could be either `get` or `post`. You should use `get`, which is the default, only when the form data is small (a few hundred characters), not sensitive (it doesn't matter if someone else sees it) and there are no files in the form. These requirements exist because when using `get`, all the form data will be appended to the current URL as encoded parameters before being sent. In our example, the chosen method is `post` because one of our input fields is a password and we don't want other people looking into our password. A good use case for using the `get` method would be with search forms. For example:

```
<!-- example 2 -->
<form action='.'>
<input type='search' name='search' />
</form>
```

In `example 2`, we have a simple search form. If we fill the `name` input with the search term `SearchItem` and hit *Enter*, the URL will look like this:

`http://mydomain.com/?search=SearchItem`

The preceding URL would then be saved into the browser history and anyone with access to it would be able to see what the previous user was searching for. In the case of sensitive data, that's bad.

Anyway, back to *example 1*. The second attribute, `action`, is useful for telling the browser which URL should receive and respond to the form data. We used `'.'` as its value because we want the form data to be sent to the current URL.

The next two lines are our input fields. Input fields are used to collect user data and, contrary to what the name may suggest, an input field may be an `input`, `textarea`, or `select` element. When using input fields, always remember to name them with the attribute `name` as it facilitates handling them in the Web application.

In the third line we have a special input field, which does not necessarily have any data to be sent, the Submit input button. By default, a form will be sent if you press *Enter* while an `input` element has focus or when a Submit button is pressed. Our *example 1* is the latter.

Wow! Finally, our form is written and explained. For an extensive list of possible types for an input field, take a look at `http://www.w3schools.com/tags/tag_input.asp`.

Handling forms

Now let's see how to integrate our form from *example 1* with an application:

```
# coding:utf-8

from flask import Flask, render_template, request

app = Flask(__name__)


@app.route('/', methods=['get', 'post'])
def login_view():
    # the methods that handle requests are called views, in flask
    msg = ''

    # form is a dictionary like attribute that holds the form data
    if request.method == 'POST':
      username = request.form["username"]
        passwd = request.form["passwd"]

        # static useless validation
        if username == 'you' and passwd == 'flask':
            msg = 'Username and password are correct'
        else:
            msg = 'Username or password are incorrect'
    return render_template('form.html', message=msg)

if __name__=='__main__':
    app.run()
```

In the preceding example, we define a view called `login_view` that accepts `get` or `post` requests; when the request is `post` (we ignore the form if it was sent by a `get` request), we fetch the values for `username` and `passwd`; then we run a very simple validation and change the value of `msg` accordingly.

 Beware: a view, in Flask, is not the same as a view in MVC. In Flask, a view is the component that receives a request and returns a response, which may be a function or a class.

Did you see the `request` variable we are handling in our example? That's a proxy to the current active `request` context. That's why `request.form` points to the sent form data.

Now, what if you're receiving a parameter encoded in the URL? How will you get it, given that the request URL is `http://localhost:5000/?page=10`?

```
# inside a flask view
def some_view():
    try:
        page = int(request.args.get('page', 1))
        assert page == 10
    except ValueError:
        page = 1
    ...
```

The preceding example is pretty common when paginating. Just as before, `request.args` is related to the current user request only. Easy!

So far, we have handled form validation pretty poorly with inline validation. No more! Let's try something fancier from now on.

WTForms and you

WTForms (`https://github.com/wtforms/wtforms`) is a standalone robust form handling library that allows you to generate HTML forms from form-like classes, implement fields and form validation, *and* include cross-source forgery protection (a nasty vulnerability that crackers may try to exploit in your Web applications). We certainly don't want that!

First, to install WTForms library, use the following:

```
pip install wtforms
```

Now let's write some forms. A WTForms form is a class that extends the Form class. As plain as that! Let's create a login form that could be used with our previous login example:

```
from wtforms import Form, StringField, PasswordField
class LoginForm(Form):
    username = StringField(u'Username:')
    passwd = PasswordField(u'Password:')
```

In the preceding code, we have a form with two fields, username and passwd, with no validation. It is just enough to build a form in a template, like this:

```
<form method='post'>
{% for field in form %}
    {{ field.label }}
    {{ field }}
    {% if field.errors %}
        {% for error in field.errors %}
            <div class="field_error">{{ error }}</div>
        {% endfor %}
    {% endif %}
{% endfor %}
</form>
```

As seen in the preceding code, you can iterate over the fields of a WTForms form and each field has a few useful attributes you can use to make your HTML look good, such as label and errors. {{ field }} will render a plain HTML input element for you. There are cases where you may want to set special attributes for the input element—for example, required, which tells your browser that the given field should not be submitted if empty. Call field as a function in order to achieve that, like so:

```
{% if field.flags.required %}
{{ field(required='required') }}
{% endif %}
```

You could pass any desired argument, as placeholder or alt, in line with the example. Flask-Empty (https://github.com/italomaia/flask-empty) has a nice example within its macros.

WTForms uses a flag system in order to allow you to check when some validations are applied to a field. If a field has a "required" validation rule, a required flag would be set to true in the fields.flags attribute. But how does WTForms validation work?

In Flask, a validator is a callable you add to your `validators` field, or a class method in the format `validate_<field>(form, field)`. It allows you to validate that the field data is as required or it raises a `ValidationError` explaining what went wrong. Let's see how our nice login form example would look with some validation:

```
# coding:utf-8
from wtforms import Form, ValidationError
from wtforms import StringField, PasswordField
from wtforms.validators import Length, InputRequired
from werkzeug.datastructures import MultiDict

import re

def is_proper_username(form, field):
    if not re.match(r"^\w+$", field.data):
        msg = '%s should have any of these characters only: a-z0-
            9_' % field.name
        raise ValidationError(msg)


class LoginForm(Form):
    username = StringField(
        u'Username:', [InputRequired(), is_proper_username,
            Length(min=3, max=40)])
    password = PasswordField(
        u'Password:', [InputRequired(), Length(min=5, max=12)])

    @staticmethod
    def validate_password(form, field):
        data = field.data
        if not re.findall('.*[a-z].*', data):
            msg = '%s should have at least one lowercase
                character' % field.name
            raise ValidationError(msg)
        # has at least one uppercase character
        if not re.findall('.*[A-Z].*', data):
            msg = '%s should have at least one uppercase
                character' % field.name
            raise ValidationError(msg)
        # has at least one number
        if not re.findall('.*[0-9].*', data):
            msg = '%s should have at least one number' %
                field.name
            raise ValidationError(msg)
        # has at least one special character
```

```
        if not re.findall('.*[^ a-zA-Z0-9].*', data):
            msg = '%s should have at least one special character'
                % field.name
            raise ValidationError(msg)

# testing our form
form = LoginForm(MultiDict([('username', 'italomaia'),
    ('password', '1L2m@msbb')]))
print form.validate()
print form.errors
```

In the preceding code, we have a full form example, with validation, using classes, methods and functions as validators and a simple test. The first argument for each of our fields is the field label. The second argument is a list of validators you want run when the `form.validate` method is called (that's pretty much what `form.validate` does). Each field validator is run sequentially, raising a `ValidationError` (and stopping the validation chain call) if an error is found.

Each validator receives the form and field as arguments and must do the validating *thing* with them. As seen with `validate_password`, which is called for the field `password` because of the naming convention. `field.data` holds the field input, so you can just validate that most of the time.

Let's understand each validator:

- `Length`: This validates that the input value length is within a given range (min, max).
- `InputRequired`: This validates that the field received a value, any value.
- `is_proper_username`: This validates that the field value matches a given regex. (There is also a built-in validator to match a regex to a given value, called **Regexp**. You should try it.)
- `validate_password`: This validates that the field value matches a given group of regex rules.

In our example test, you may have noticed the use of a special dictionary-like class called `MultiDict` from the `werkzeug` library. It is used because the `formdata` parameter, which may receive your `request.form` or `request.args`, must be a `multidict-type`. It pretty much means you can't use a plain dictionary here.

When `form.validate` is called, all the validators are called. First the field validators, then the `class` method field validators; `form.errors` is a dictionary populated with all the field errors found after validate is called. You can then iterate over it to show what you found in your templates, console, and so on.

Flask-WTF

Flask uses extensions in order to integrate transparently with third party libraries. WTForms with Flask-WTF is a good example of that as we will soon see. And, by the way, a Flask extension is a piece of code that integrates its configuration, context, and usage with Flask in a predictable way. That means extension usage is pretty similar. Now make sure Flask-WTF is installed in your virtual environment before continuing:

```
# oh god, so hard... not!

pip flask-wtf
```

From http://flask-wtf.readthedocs.org/, the project website, we have the following list of features offered by Flask-WTF:

- Integration with WTForms
- Secure form with a CSRF token
- File upload that works with Flask-Uploads
- Global CSRF protection
- Recaptcha support
- Internationalization integration

We'll see the first two features in this chapter while the third will be discussed in *Chapter 10, What Now?*. The last three features will not be covered in this book. We advise you to explore them as homework.

Integration with WTForms

Flask-WTF uses a little trick regarding `request` in order to integrate. As `request` implements a proxy to your current request and request data, and it is available whenever you're inside a `request` context, the extension `Form` will just grab the `request.form` data by default, saving you some typing.

Our `login_view` example could be rewritten taking into account what was discussed so far, like this:

```
# make sure you're importing Form from flask_wtf and not wtforms
from flask_wtf import Form

# --//--
@app.route('/', methods=['get', 'post'])
def login_view():
    # the methods that handle requests are called views, in flask
    msg = ''
```

```
# request.form is passed implicitly; implies POST
form = LoginForm()
# if the form should also deal with form.args, do it like
    this:
# form = LoginForm(request.form or request.args)

# checks that the submit method is POST and form is valid
if form.validate_on_submit():
    msg = 'Username and password are correct'
else:
    msg = 'Username or password are incorrect'
return render_template('form.html', message=msg)
```

We could go even further, as we are, obviously, perfectionists:

```
# flash allows us to send messages to the user template without
# altering the returned context
from flask import flash
from flask import redirect
@app.route('/', methods=['get', 'post'])
def login_view():
    # msg is no longer necessary. We will use flash, instead
    form = LoginForm()

    if form.validate_on_submit():
        flash(request, 'Username and password are correct')
        # it's good practice to redirect after a successful form
            submit
        return redirect('/')
    return render_template('form.html', form=form)
```

In the template, exchange {{ message }} by:

```
{#
beautiful example from
http://flask.pocoo.org/docs/0.10/patterns/flashing/#simple-flashing
#}
{% with messages = get_flashed_messages() %}
  {% if messages %}
    <ul class='messages'>
    {% for message in messages %}
      <li>{{ message }}</li>
    {% endfor %}
    </ul>
  {% endif %}
{% endwith %}
```

`get_flashed_messages` is available in the template context by default and gives you all the flashed messages for the current user that have not yet been shown. We then cache it with `with`, check whether it is not empty, then iterate over it.

 Flashed messages are especially useful when redirecting, because they are not bound to the response context.

Securing forms with a CSRF token

Cross Site Request Forgery (**CSRF**) happens when a site tries to exploit the trust another site has on your browser (given you're the user). Basically, a site you're visiting will try to get, or alter information of, a site you have already visited and authenticated. Imagine you're visiting a website and that website has an image that loads a URL from another website you've already authenticated with; imagine that the given URL requests an action of the former website and that action changes something from your account—for example, its status is amended to inactive. Well, that's a simple case of a CSRF attack. Another common case is when a JSONP request is sent. If the attacked site, the one you're not visiting, accepts JSONP form substitution (JSONP is used for cross-domain requests) and does not have CRSF protection, well, then you'll have an even nastier attack.

WTForms come with its own CSRF protection; Flask-WTF just glues the whole thing together with Flask, making your life easier. In order to have CSRF protection while using the extension, you need to have `secret_key` set, and that's it:

```
app.secret_key = 'some secret string value' # ex: import os;
    os.urandom(24)
```

Then, whenever you write a form that should have CSRF protection, just make sure to add the CSRF token to it, like this:

```
<form method='post'>{{ form.csrf_token }}
{% for field in form if field.name != 'csrf_token' %}
    <div class="field">
    {{ field.label }} {{ field }}
    </div>
    {% if field.errors %}
        {% for error in field.errors %}
        <div class="field_error">{{ error }}</div>
        {% endfor %}
    {% endif %}
{% endfor %}
<input type='submit' />
</form>
```

When the form is received, the CSRF token is checked against what is registered in the user session. If they match, the form's source is good. This is a safe approach because a website cannot read a cookie set by another website.

In cases when you don't want CSRF protection in a form, do not add the token. You will have to turn off the CSRF protection for the form if you wish to unprotect it, like this:

```
form = Form(csrf_enabled=False)
```

You *may* need to unprotect a form in the case of search fields that use the `get` method but are also validated with a Form.

Challenges

Create a Web application that receives a name and then answers: `"Hello <NAME>"`. If the form is sent empty, an error message should be displayed. If the name given is "Chuck Norris", the answer should be "Roundhouse KICK!".

Create a Web application that shows an image and asks the user what he sees. The application should then validate if the answer is correct. If it is not, show the user an error message. Otherwise, congratulate the user and show a new image. Use Flask-WTF.

Create a calculator with the four operations. It should have all the numbers and operators for the user to click on. Make sure it looks like a calculator (because we are perfectionists!) and complains if the user tries something evil, such as dividing 0 by 0.

Summary

So much learned... What can I say! No harm trying, right? Well, we have seen how to write HTML forms; read forms with Flask; write WTForms forms; validate form data with plain Python and form validators; and write custom validators. We also saw how to use Flask-WTF to write and validate our forms and how to protect our applications against CSRF attacks.

In the next chapter, we'll look at how to store our Web application data in relational and non-relational databases using great, easy-to-use libraries and how to integrate them with Flask. A brief overview on databases will also take place to make for smoother knowledge absorption.

5
Where Do You Store Your Stuff?

I'm like a squirrel. Once in a while, I leave money in secret stashes around the house in case I get mugged or just spend too much in a month. I truly forget where all my stashes are, and that is kind of funny and sad (for me).

Now, imagine you're storing something equally important or even more important than money, for instance, client data or even your company data. Could you allow yourself to store it in places that could later be lost or accessible to someone who could meddle with your "stash"? We are in the information era; information is power!

In the web application world, we have two big players for data storage: **relational databases** and **NoSQL databases**. The first is the traditional way where your data is stored inside tables and columns and where transactions matter, ACID is expected and normalization is the key (pun intended)! It uses **SQL** to store and retrieve data. In the second way, things get a little wild. Your data may be stored in different structures such as documents, graphs, key value mappings, and others. Writing and consulting languages are vendor-specific, and you may have to give up on ACID too in a tradeoff for speed, lots of speed!

You have probably guessed it already! This chapter is all about the **M** layer of **MVC**, that is, how to store and access your data in a transparent way with Flask! We'll look at the examples of how to use query and write to both the database types, and when to choose which one to use.

 ACID is the acronym for atomicity, consistency, isolation, and durability. Refer to http://en.wikipedia.org/ wiki/ACID for a cozy definition and overview.

SQLAlchemy

SQLAlchemy is an amazing library for working with relational databases. It was made by the Pocoo Team, the same folks that brought you Flask, and is considered "The Facto" Python SQL library. It works with SQLite, Postgres, MySQL, Oracle, and all SQL databases, which comes with compatible drivers.

SQLite describes itself as a self-contained, serverless, zero-configuration, and transactional SQL database engine (`https://sqlite.org/about.html`). One of its main goals is to be a great embeddable database solution for applications and small devices, which it is! It is also very easy to use and that makes it perfect for our learning purposes.

Though all the examples will be given and tested with SQLite in mind, they should work in the other databases with little to no changes. Database-specific tips will be given from time to time whenever appropriate.

Refer to `http://www.w3schools.com/sql/default.asp` for an extensive SQL reference.

Before our first example, should we review a few relational database concepts?

Concepts

Tables are low-level abstraction structures where your data is stored. It is made up of **columns** and **rows**, where each column represents a part of your data and each row represents a full record. Usually, each table represents a low-level abstraction of a class model.

Rows are individual records of a given class model. You may need to scatter multiple row records across different tables to record a full piece of information. A good example is an **MxN relationship**.

Columns represent the stored data itself. Each column has a specific type, and accepts only that type as input data. You may think of it as an abstraction of a class model attribute.

Transactions are how you group the operations you want to be executed together. It is used mainly to achieve atomicity. This way, no operations are done halfway.

Primary key is a database concept where part of a record's data is used to identify the given record across the database table. It is usually implemented by the database through constraints.

Foreign key is a database concept where a set of data is used to identify a given record across tables. Its main use is to construct relationships between rows in different tables. It is usually implemented by the database through constraints.

One main concern when working with relational databases is data normalization. In relational databases, related data is stored across different tables. You may have a table to hold a person's data, a table for the person's address, another for his/her cars, and so on.

Each table is isolated from one another and the related data may be retrievable, thanks to the relations established by the foreign keys! The data normalization techniques are a set of rules used to allow proper scattering of the data across the tables so that the related tables are easily fetched and redundancy is kept to a minimum.

Please, refer to `http://en.wikipedia.org/wiki/Database_normalization` for an overview of database normalization.

For an overview of the normal forms, please refer to the following links:

`http://en.wikipedia.org/wiki/First_normal_form`

`http://en.wikipedia.org/wiki/Second_normal_form`

`http://en.wikipedia.org/wiki/Third_normal_form`

We may now proceed!

Hands on

Let's begin by installing the library into our environment and trying out a few examples:

```
pip install sqlalchemy
```

On to our first example! Let's create a simple employee database for a company (maybe yours?):

```
from sqlalchemy import create_engine
db = create_engine('sqlite:///employees.sqlite')
# echo output to console
db.echo = True

conn = db.connect()

conn.execute("""
CREATE TABLE employee (
```

```
   id           INTEGER PRIMARY KEY,
   name         STRING(100) NOT NULL,
   birthday     DATE NOT NULL
)""")

conn.execute("INSERT INTO employee VALUES (NULL, 'marcos mango',
   date('1990-09-06') );")
conn.execute("INSERT INTO employee VALUES (NULL, 'rosie rinn',
   date('1980-09-06') );")
conn.execute("INSERT INTO employee VALUES (NULL, 'mannie moon',
   date('1970-07-06') );")
for row in conn.execute("SELECT * FROM employee"):
    print row
# give connection back to the connection pool
conn.close()
```

The preceding example is pretty simple. We create a SQLAlchemy engine, grab a connection from the **connection pool** (engine handles that for you) and then we execute the SQL command to create a table, insert a few rows and query to see whether everything occurred as expected.

Visit http://en.wikipedia.org/wiki/ Connection_pool for the connection pool pattern overview. (This is important, really!)

In our insertion, we provided the value NULL to the primary key id. Be aware that SQLite will not populate the primary key with NULL; instead, it will ignore the NULL value and set the column with a new, unique, across the table integer. That's SQLite- specific behavior. **Oracle**, for example, would require you to insert a sequence's next value explicitly in order to set a new unique column value for the primary key.

Our preceding example uses a feature called **autocommit**. It means each execute method call commits to the database immediately. In this way, you could not execute multiple statements at once, a common scenario in real world applications.

To execute multiple statements at once, we should use **transactions**. We could rewrite our previous example with transactions in order to make sure all three insertions are either committed together or not at all (grim look...):

```
# we start our transaction here
# all actions now are executed within the transaction context
trans = conn.begin()

try:
```

```
    # we are using a slightly different insertion syntax for
convenience, here;
    # id value is not explicitly provided
    conn.execute("INSERT INTO employee (name, birthday) VALUES
        ('marcos mango', date('1990-09-06') );")
    conn.execute("INSERT INTO employee (name, birthday) VALUES
        ('rosie rinn', date('1980-09-06') );")
    conn.execute("INSERT INTO employee (name, birthday) VALUES
        ('mannie moon', date('1970-07-06') );")
    # commit all
    trans.commit()
except:
    # all or nothing. Undo what was executed within the transaction
    trans.rollback()
    raise
```

Nothing fancy so far. In our example, we create a transaction from the connection, execute a few statements and then commit it to finish the transaction. If an error occurs between the beginning and end of a transaction, the `except` block will be reached and all the statements executed within the transaction will rollback or "undone".

We can make our example complete by creating a relation among the tables. Imagine our employee has one or more addresses registered with his/her company profile. We will create a 1xN relation, where an employee may have one, or more addresses.

```
# coding:utf-8
from sqlalchemy import create_engine

engine = create_engine('sqlite:///employees.sqlite')
engine.echo = True

conn = engine.connect()

conn.execute("""
CREATE TABLE employee (
  id          INTEGER PRIMARY KEY,
  name        STRING(100) NOT NULL,
  birthday    DATE NOT NULL
) """)

conn.execute("""
CREATE TABLE address(
  id       INTEGER PRIMARY KEY,
  street   STRING(100) NOT NULL,
  number   INTEGER,
  google_maps STRING(255),
  id_employee INTEGER NOT NULL,
```

```
        FOREIGN KEY(id_employee) REFERENCES employee(id)
    ) """)

    trans = conn.begin()
    try:
        conn.execute("INSERT INTO employee (name, birthday) VALUES
            ('marcos mango', date('1990-09-06') );")
        conn.execute("INSERT INTO employee (name, birthday) VALUES
            ('rosie rinn', date('1980-09-06') );")
        conn.execute("INSERT INTO employee (name, birthday) VALUES
            ('mannie moon', date('1970-07-06') );")
        # insert addresses for each employee
        conn.execute(
            "INSERT INTO address (street, number, google_maps,
                id_employee) "
            "VALUES ('Oak', 399, '', 1)")
        conn.execute(
            "INSERT INTO address (street, number, google_maps,
                id_employee) "
            "VALUES ('First Boulevard', 1070, '', 1)")
        conn.execute(
            "INSERT INTO address (street, number, google_maps,
                id_employee) "
            "VALUES ('Cleveland, OH', 10,
                'Cleveland,+OH,+USA/@41.4949426,-81.70586,11z', 2)")
        trans.commit()
    except:
        trans.rollback()
        raise

    # get marcos mango addresses
    for row in conn.execute("""
      SELECT a.street, a.number FROM employee e
      LEFT OUTER JOIN address a
      ON e.id = a.id_employee
      WHERE e.name like '%marcos%';
      """):
        print "address:", row
    conn.close()
```

In our new and updated, awesome example, we record some addresses of our employees, making sure to use the correct value for the foreign keys (id_employee) and then we look out for the addresses of an employee called 'marcos mango' using LEFT JOIN.

We have seen how to create tables and relations, run statements to consult and insert data, and use transactions with SQLAlchemy; we're yet to explore much of the library power within SQLAlchemy.

SQLAlchemy has a built-in ORM, which allows you to work with database tables as if they were native object instances. Imagine reading a column value as if it was an instance attribute or consulting a complex table relation through a method, that's SQLAlchemy's ORM.

Let's see how our example will look using the built-in ORM:

```
# coding:utf-8

from sqlalchemy import create_engine
from sqlalchemy import Column, Integer, String, Date, ForeignKey
from sqlalchemy.orm import sessionmaker, relationship, backref
from sqlalchemy.ext.declarative import declarative_base

from datetime import datetime

engine = create_engine('sqlite:///employees.sqlite')
engine.echo = True

# base class for our models
Base = declarative_base()

# we create a session binded to our engine
Session = sessionmaker(bind=engine)

# and then the session itself
session = Session()

# our first model
class Address(Base):
    # the table name we want in the database
    __tablename__ = 'address'

    # our primary key
    id = Column(Integer, primary_key=True)
    street = Column(String(100))
    number = Column(Integer)
    google_maps = Column(String(255))
    # our foreign key to employee
    id_employee = Column(Integer, ForeignKey('employee.id'))
```

```
    def __repr__(self):
        return u"%s, %d" % (self.street, self.number)


class Employee(Base):
    __tablename__ = 'employee'

    id = Column(Integer, primary_key=True)
    name = Column(String(100))
    birthday = Column(Date)
    # we map
    addresses = relationship("Address", backref="employee")

    def __repr__(self):
        return self.name

# create our database from our classes
Base.metadata.create_all(engine)

# execute everything inside a transaction
session.add_all([
        Employee(name='marcos mango',
            birthday=datetime.strptime('1990-09-06', '%Y-%m-%d')),
        Employee(name='rosie rinn',
            birthday=datetime.strptime('1980-09-06', '%Y-%m-%d')),
        Employee(name='mannie moon',
            birthday=datetime.strptime('1970-07-06', '%Y-%m-%d'))
    ])
session.commit()

session.add_all([
    Address(street='Oak', number=399, google_maps='',
        id_employee=1),
    Address(street='First Boulevard', number=1070, google_maps='',
        id_employee=1),
    Address(street='Cleveland, OH', number=10,
            google_maps='Cleveland,+OH,+USA/@41.4949426,-
                81.70586,11z', id_employee=2)
])
session.commit()

# get marcos, then his addresses
marcos = session.query(Employee).filter
    (Employee.name.like(r"%marcos%")).first()
for address in marcos.addresses:
    print 'Address:', address
```

The preceding example has quite a few concepts to be introduced. First, we create our engine, the SQLAlchemy engine used in the first example, then we create our base model class. While `Employee` will be mapped into a table called `employee` by `create_all`, each defined `Column` attribute will be mapped into a column of the given table in the database with the proper constraints. For the `id` field, for example, it is defined as a primary key, so it will have the primary key constraint created for it. The `id_employee` is a foreign key, which is a reference to the primary key of another table, so it will have a foreign key constraint, and so on.

All of our class models should inherit from it. Then we create a `session`. A session is how you work with the SQLAlchemy ORM models.

Sessions have an internal ongoing transaction, so it's very simple for it to have a *transaction-like* behavior. It also maps your models to the correct engine in case you're using more than one; but wait, there's more! It also keeps track of all the model instances loaded in/from it. For example, if you add a model instance to it and then modify that very instance, the session is smart enough to acknowledge the change of one of its objects. It will, thus, mark itself as dirty (stuff was changed) until a commit or rollback is called.

In the example, after finding marcos, we could change "Marcos Mango's" name to something else, such as `"marcos tangerine"`, like this:

```
marcos.name = "marcos tangerine"
session.commit()
```

Now, comment the whole code after `Base.metadata` and add the following:

```
marcos = session.query(Employee).
    filter(Employee.name.like(r"%marcos%")).first()
marcos_last_name = marcos.name.split(' ')[-1]
print marcos_last_name
```

Now, re-execute the example. Marcos new last name now is "tangerine". Magical!

 For an amazing, super duper, mega power reference on querying with SQLAlchemy ORM, please visit `http://docs.sqlalchemy.org/en/rel_0_9/orm/ tutorial.html#querying`.

After so much talk about SQLAlchemy, could you please wake up as we'll talk about Flask-SQLAlchemy, the extension that integrates the library with Flask.

Flask-SQLAlchemy

Flask-SQLAlchemy is a thin extension that wraps SQLAlchemy around Flask. It allows you to configure the SQLAlchemy engine through your configuration file and binds a session to each request, giving you a transparent way to handle transactions. Let's see how to do all that. First, let's make sure we have all the necessary packages installed. With the virtual environment loaded, run:

```
pip install flask-wtf flask-sqlalchemy
```

Our code should look like this:

```python
# coding:utf-8
from flask import Flask, render_template, redirect, flash
from flask_wtf import Form
from flask.ext.sqlalchemy import SQLAlchemy

from wtforms.ext.sqlalchemy.orm import model_form

app = Flask(__name__)
app.config['SECRET_KEY'] = 'secret'
app.config['SQLALCHEMY_DATABASE_URI'] =
    'sqlite:////tmp/employees.sqlite'
app.config['SQLALCHEMY_ECHO'] = True

# initiate the extension
db = SQLAlchemy(app)


# define our model
class Employee(db.Model):
    __tablename__ = 'employee'

    id = db.Column(db.Integer, primary_key=True)
    name = db.Column(db.String(100), nullable=False)
    birthday = db.Column(db.Date, nullable=False)

    def __repr__(self):
        return 'employee %s' % self.name

# create the database
db.create_all()

# auto-generate form for our model
EmployeeForm = model_form(Employee, base_class=Form, field_args={
```

```
        'name': {
        'class': 'employee'
    }
})


@app.route("/", methods=['GET', 'POST'])
def index():
    # as you remember, request.POST is implicitly provided as argument
    form = EmployeeForm()

    try:
        if form.validate_on_submit():
            employee = Employee()
            form.populate_obj(employee)
            db.session.add(employee)
            db.session.commit()
            flash('New employee add to database')
            return redirect('/')
    except Exception, e:
        # log e
        db.session.rollback()
        flash('An error occurred accessing the database. Please,
            contact administration.')

    employee_list=Employee.query.all()
    return render_template('index.html', form=form,
        employee_list=employee_list)

if __name__ == '__main__':
    app.debug = True
    app.run()
```

The preceding example is pretty complete. It has a form validation, CSRF protection, auto-generated form from model, and database integration. Let's focus only on what we have not mentioned so far.

The auto form generation is pretty handy. Using model_form, you're able to introspect the defined model class and generate a form class fit for that model. You may also provide arguments to the fields through the model_form parameter field_args, which is pretty useful for adding element classes or extra validators.

You may have also noticed that Employee extends db.Model which is your ORM model base class. All your models should extend it in order to be known by db, which encapsulates our engine and holds our request aware session.

Inside the index function, we instantiate the form, then check whether it was submitted through POST and is valid. Inside the `if` block, we instantiate our employee model and use `populate_obj` to put the values of the form inside the model instance. We could also do it field by field, like this:

```
employee.name = form.name.data
employee. birthday = form.birthday.data
```

The `populate_obj` is just more convenient. After populating the model, we add it to the session to keep track of it and commit the session. In case of any exception in this block, we have it inside a try/except block with a rollback prepared.

Note that we use `Employee.query` to consult which employees are stored in our database. Each model class comes with a `query` attribute that allows you to fetch and filter results from the database. Each filter call to `query` will return a `BaseQuery` instance, which allows you to stack your filters, like this:

```
queryset = Employee.query.filter_by(name='marcos mango')
queryset = queryset.filter_by(birthday=datetime.strptime('1990-09-06',
'%Y-%m-%d'))
queryset.all()  # <= returns the result of both filters applied
together
```

The possibilities here are many. Why don't you try a few examples on your own now?

> The most common security problem related to web applications and databases is the **SQL Injection Attack**, where an attacker injects SQL instructions into your queries to the database, gaining privileges he/she should not have. The SQLAlchemy's engine object "auto-magically" escapes special characters in your consults; so, unless you explicitly bypass its quoting mechanism, you should be safe.

MongoDB

MongoDB is a widely used, powerful NoSQL database. It allows you to store your data inside documents; a mutable, dictionary-like, object-like structure where your data may be stored without you worrying about things such as "is my data normalized to the third normal form?" or "do I have to create another table to store my relation?", and others.

MongoDB documents are actually BSON documents, a superset of JSON with extended data type support. If you know how to handle JSON documents, you should have no problem.

If JSON means nothing to you, just take a look at `http://www.w3schools.com/json/`.

Let's install MongoDB locally in order to try out some examples:

```
sudo apt-get install mongodb
```

Now, from console, type:

```
mongo
```

You'll enter the MongoDB interactive console. From it, you may execute commands, add documents to your database, query, update, or remove. Anything you can achieve grammatically, you may also achieve through the console. Now, let's understand the two important MongoDB concepts: databases and collections.

Inside MongoDB, your documents are grouped inside collections, while collections are grouped inside databases. So, after connecting to MongoDB, the first thing you should do is to choose which database you plan to use. You do not need to create the database, connecting to it is enough to create the database. The same case is applicable for the collections. You also do not need to define your document structure prior to using it, nor are you required to implement complex altering commands if you decide your documents structure should change. Here's an example:

```
> use example
switched to db example
> db.employees.insert({name: 'marcos mango', birthday: new
  Date('Sep 06, 1990')})
WriteResult({ "nInserted" : 1 })
> db.employees.find({'name': {$regex: /marcos/}})
```

In the preceding code, we switch to the example database, then we insert a new document into the employees collection (we do not need to create it before use) and eventually, we search for it using a regular expression. The MongoDB console is actually a JavaScript console, so new `Date` is actually the JavaScript class `Date` being instantiated. It's very simple.

 If you're not familiar with JavaScript, visit `http://www.w3schools.com/js/default.asp` for a nice overview.

We can store inside any JSON-type documents, also a few others. Visit `http://docs.mongodb.org/manual/reference/bson-types/` for the full list.

Regarding proper usage of MongoDB, just keep a few golden rules in mind:

- Avoid keeping data from one collection to another as MongoDB does not *like* joins

- Having document values as lists is OK in MongoDB, even expected

- Proper document indexes (not covered in this book) are key to good performance in MongoDB

- Writes are much slower than reads and may affect overall performance

MongoEngine

MongoEngine is a terrific Python library to access and manipulate MongoDB documents and uses **PyMongo**, the MongoDB recommended Python library underneath.

 As PyMongo does not have a **Document-object Mapper** (**DOM**), we are not using it directly. Nonetheless, there will be cases where the MongoEngine API will not be enough and you'll need to use PyMongo to achieve your goal.

It has its own consulting API and document to class mapper that allows you to work with the documents in a similar way you would work with SQLAlchemy ORM. That's a good thing because MongoDB is schema-less. It does not enforce the schema as a relational database would do. That way you don't have to declare how your document should look like before using it. MongoDB just doesn't care!

In actual daily development, knowing exactly what kind of information you're supposed to store in a document is a great anti-madness feature and MongoEngine gives it to you out of the box.

As you already have MongoDB on your machine, just install the MongoEngine library to start coding with it:

```
pip install mongoengine pymongo==2.8
```

Let's add "Rosie Rinn" to the database using our new library:

```
# coding:utf-8

from mongoengine import *
from datetime import datetime

# as the mongo daemon, mongod, is running locally, we just need the
database name to connect
```

```
connect('example')


class Employee(Document):
    name = StringField()
    birthday = DateTimeField()

    def __unicode__(self):
        return u'employee %s' % self.name

employee = Employee()
employee.name = 'rosie rinn'
employee.birthday = datetime.strptime('1980-09-06', '%Y-%m-%d')
employee.save()

for e in Employee.objects(name__contains='rosie'):
    print e
```

Understanding our example: first, we create a MongoDB connection with the `example` database, then define our employee document just like we did with SQLAlchemy, and eventually, we insert our employee "Rosie" and query to see whether everything is OK.

When declaring our `Employee` class, you may have noticed we had to define each field with its proper field type. If MongoDB is schema-less, why is that? MongoEngine enforces the type of each model field. If you had `IntField` defined for your model and provided it a string value, MongoEngine would raise a validation error as that is not a proper field value. Also, we defined a __unicode__ method for `Employee` in order to have it print the employee's name in our loop. The __repr__ will not work here.

As MongoDB does not support transactions (MongoDB is not ACID, remember?), neither does MongoEngine, every operation we do is atomic. As we create our "Rosie" and call the `save` method, "Rosie" is inserted in the database at once; there is no need to commit the changes or anything like that.

At last, we have the database consult where we search for "Rosie". To query a chosen collection, you should use the `objects` handler available in every MongoEngine document. It exposes a Django-like interface for querying with support to operations such as `contains`, `icontains`, `ne`, `lte`, and others. For a full list of query operators, visit `https://mongoengine-odm.readthedocs.org/guide/querying.html#query-operators`.

Flask-MongoEngine

MongoEngine is pretty easy by itself, but someone thought things could go better, and there we have Flask-MongoEngine. It gives you three main features:

- Flask-DebugToolbar Integration (weeee!)
- Django-like querysets (`get_or_404`, `first_or_404`, `paginate`, `paginate_field`)
- Connection management

Flask-DebugToolbar is a neat Flask extension inspired by the Django-DebugToolbar extension that keeps track of what is happening inside your application behind the hood, such as HTTP headers used in a request, CPU time, number of active MongoDB connections, and others.

The Django-like queries are a helpful feature as they allow you to avoid some boring coding here and there. The `get_or_404(*args, **kwargs)` query method will raise a 404 HTTP page if the document being looking for is not found (it uses a `get`, internally). In case you're building a blog, you might like to use this little fellow while loading a specific post entry. The `first_or_404()` query method is similar, but works with the collection. If the collection is empty, it raises a 404 HTTP page. The `paginate(page, per_page)` query is actually a very helpful query method. It provides you with a pagination interface out of the box. It will not work well with huge collections because MongoDB requires a different strategy in these cases, but most of the time, it will be all you need. The `paginate_field(field_name, doc_id, page, per_page)` is a more specific version of paginate as you'll be paginating through a single document field and not a collection. It is very useful when you have a document where one of the fields is a huge list.

Now, let's look at a full example with `flask-mongoengine`. First, let's install the library in our virtual environment:

```
pip install flask-mongoengine
```

Now on to coding:

```python
# coding:utf-8

from flask import Flask, flash, redirect, render_template
from flask.ext.mongoengine import MongoEngine
from flask.ext.mongoengine.wtf import model_form
from flask_wtf import Form

app = Flask(__name__)
app.config['SECRET_KEY'] = 'secret'
app.config['MONGODB_SETTINGS'] = {
    # 'replicaset': '',
```

```python
    'db': 'example',
    # 'host': '',
    # 'username': '',
    # 'password': ''
}
db = MongoEngine(app)


class Employee(db.Document):
    name = db.StringField()
    # mongoengine does not support datefield
    birthday = db.DateTimeField()

    def __unicode__(self):
        return u'employee %s' % self.name


# auto-generate form for our model
EmployeeForm = model_form(Employee, base_class=Form, field_args={
    'birthday': {
        # we want to use date format, not datetime
        'format': '%Y-%m-%d'
    }
})


@app.route("/", methods=['GET', 'POST'])
def index():
    # as you remember, request.POST is implicitly provided as argument
    form = EmployeeForm()

    try:
        if form.validate_on_submit():
            employee = Employee()
            form.populate_obj(employee)
            employee.save()
            flash('New employee add to database')
            return redirect('/')
    except:
        # log e
        flash('An error occurred accessing the database. Please,
            contact administration.')

    employee_list=Employee.objects()
    return render_template('index.html', form=form,
        employee_list=employee_list)

if __name__ == '__main__':
    app.debug = True
    app.run()
```

Our Flask-MongoEngine example is pretty similar to our Flask-SQLAlchemy example. Besides differences in the imports, there is the MongoDB configuration, as MongoDB requires different parameters; we have the `birthday` field type as MongoEngine does not support `DateField`; there is birthday format overwrite as the default string format for `datetimefield` is different than what we want; and we have the changes in the `index` method.

As we do not have to handle sessions with Flask-MongoEngine, we just remove all references to it. We also change how `employee_list` is built.

 As MongoDB does not parse the data you send to it in an attempt to figure out what the query is about, you do not have SQL injection-like problems with it.

Relational versus NoSQL

You might be wondering when to use relational and when to use NoSQL. Well, given the techniques and technologies in existence today, I would recommend you work with the type you feel better working with. NoSQL brags about being schema-less, scalable, fast, and so on, but relational databases are also quite fast for most of your needs. A few relational databases, such as Postgres, even support documents. What about scaling? Well, most projects do not need to scale as they will never be big enough. Others, just scale with their relational database.

If there is no *important* reason to pick one or the other for native schema-less support or full ACID support, either of them will be good enough. Even security-wise, there are no big differences worth mentioning. MongoDB has its own authorization scheme as most relational databases do, and, if properly configured, both are just as secure. Usually, the application layer is more troublesome in this matter.

Summary

This chapter was pretty intense! We had an overview of relational and NoSQL databases, we learned about MongoDB and MongoEngine, SQLite and SQLAlchemy, and how to use extensions to integrate Flask with each. Knowledge is stacking up fast! You're now capable of creating more complex web applications with database support, custom validation, CSRF protection, and user communication.

In the next chapter, we'll learn about REST, its advantages, and how to create services to be consumed by your app.

6
But I Wanna REST Mom, Now!

REST is an architectural style that has been gaining momentum these last few years due to its many features and architectural constraints such as cacheability, stateless behavior, and its interface requirement.

 For a nice overview of REST architecture, refer to
http://www.drdobbs.com/Web-development/
restful-Web-services-a-tutorial/240169069
and http://en.wikipedia.org/wiki/
Representational_state_transfer.

Our focus in this chapter will be on RESTful Web Services and APIs—that is, Web services and Web APIs following the REST architecture. Let's start at the beginning: what is a Web service?

A Web service is a Web application that can be consulted by your application as if it was an API, improving the user experience. If your RESTful Web service does not need to be called from a traditional UI interface, and may be used standalone, then what you have is a **RESTful Web Service API**, "RESTful API" for short, that works just like a regular API, but through a Web server.

A call to a Web service could, for example, start a batch process, update the database, or just retrieve some data. There is no restriction imposed on what a service may perform.

RESTful Web services should be accessible through a **URI** (like a URL) and may be accessed by any Web protocol, although **HTTP** is the king here. Because of that, we'll focus on **HTTP**. Our Web service response, also called a resource, may have any desired format; as TXT, XML, or JSON, but the most common format is JSON, as it is very simple to use. We'll also focus on JSON. When using HTTP with Web services, a common practice is to use the HTTP default methods (GET, POST, PUT, DELETE, and OPTIONS) to give more information to the server about what we want to achieve. This technique allows us to have different functionality within the same service.

A service call to `http://localhost:5000/age` could return the user's age through a GET request, or remove its value through a DELETE request.

Let's see what each *usually used* method is *usually* used for:

- GET: This is used to retrieve a resource. You want information? No database update? Use GET!

- POST: This is used to insert new data into the server, such as adding a new employee in your database.

- PUT: This is used to update data on the server. You have an employee that decided to change his nickname in the system? Use PUT to do that!

- DELETE: This is your best method for getting rid of data on your server!

- OPTIONS: This is used to ask a service which methods it supports.

Lots of theory so far; let's put it into practice with a Flask-powered REST Web Service example.

First, install the required library for the example:

```
pip install marshmallow
```

Now, on to the example:

```
# coding:utf-8

from flask import Flask, jsonify
from flask.ext.sqlalchemy import SQLAlchemy

from marshmallow import Schema

app = Flask(__name__)
app.config['SECRET_KEY'] = 'secret'
app.config['SQLALCHEMY_DATABASE_URI'] =
    'sqlite:////tmp/articles.sqlite'
```

```python
db = SQLAlchemy(app)


class Article(db.Model):
    __tablename__ = 'articles'

    id = db.Column(db.Integer, primary_key=True)
    title = db.Column(db.String(100), nullable=False)
    content = db.Column(db.Text(), nullable=False)

    def __unicode__(self):
        return self.content


# we use marshmallow Schema to serialize our articles
class ArticleSchema(Schema):
    """
    Article dict serializer
    """
    class Meta:
        # which fields should be serialized?
        fields = ('id', 'title', 'content')


article_schema = ArticleSchema()
# many -> allow for object list dump
articles_schema = ArticleSchema(many=True)

@app.route("/articles/", methods=["GET"])
@app.route("/articles/<article_id>", methods=["GET"])
def articles(article_id=None):
    if article_id:
        article = Article.query.get(article_id)

        if article is None:
            return jsonify({"msgs": ["the article you're looking
                for could not be found"]}), 404

        result = article_schema.dump(article)
        return jsonify({'article': result})
    else:
        # never return the whole set! As it would be very slow
        queryset = Article.query.limit(10)
        result = articles_schema.dump(queryset)

        # jsonify serializes our dict into a proper flask response
```

```
        return jsonify({"articles": result.data})


    db.create_all()

    # let's populate our database with some data; empty examples are not
    that cool
    if Article.query.count() == 0:
        article_a = Article(title='some title', content='some
            content')
        article_b = Article(title='other title', content='other
            content')

        db.session.add(article_a)
        db.session.add(article_b)
        db.session.commit()

if __name__ == '__main__':
    # we define the debug environment only if running through command
    line
    app.config['SQLALCHEMY_ECHO'] = True
    app.debug = True
    app.run()
```

In the preceding example, we create a Web service to consult articles using a GET request. The `jsonify` function is introduced, as it is used to serialize Python objects into Flask JSON responses. We also use the marshmallow library to serialize SQLAlchemy results into Python dictionaries, as there is no native API for such.

Let's discuss the example, step-by-step:

First, we create our app and configure our SQLAlchemy extension. We then define the `Article` model, which will hold our article data, and an ArticleSchema, which allows marshmallow to serialize our articles. We have to define in the Schema Meta, which fields should be serialized. `article_schema` is our schema instance used to serialize single articles while `articles_schema` serializes article collections.

Our articles view has two routes defined, one for article listing and another for article detail, which returns a single article.

Inside it, if `article_id` is provided, we serialize and return the requested article. If `article_id` does not have a corresponding record in the database, we return a message with the given error and the HTTP code 404, indicating a "not found" status. If `article_id` is None, we serialize and return 10 articles. You might ask, Why not return all the articles in the database? If we have 10,000 articles in the database and try to return that many, our server will certainly have a problem; thus, avoid returning everything from the database.

This kind of service is usually consumed by Ajax requests made using JavaScript such as jQuery or PrototypeJS. When sending Ajax requests, these libraries add a special header that allows us to identify whether the given request is actually an Ajax request. In our preceding example, we serve the JSON response to all GET requests.

 Don't know Ajax? Visit `http://www.w3schools.com/Ajax/ajax_intro.asp`.

We could be more selective and only send JSON responses to Ajax requests. Regular requests will receive plain HTML responses. To do that, we would have to make a slight change in our view, like this:

```python
from flask import request
...

@app.route("/articles/", methods=["GET"])
@app.route("/articles/<article_id>", methods=["GET"])
def articles(article_id=None):
    if article_id:
        article = Article.query.get(article_id)

        if request.is_xhr:
            if article is None:
                return jsonify({"msgs": ["the article you're
                    looking for could not be found"]}), 404

            result = article_schema.dump(article)
            return jsonify({'article': result})
        else:
            if article is None:
                abort(404)

            return render_template('article.html',
                article=article)
    else:
        queryset = Article.query.limit(10)

        if request.is_xhr:
            # never return the whole set! As it would be very slow
            result = articles_schema.dump(queryset)

            # jsonify serializes our dict into a proper flask response
            return jsonify({"articles": result.data})
        else:
            return render_template('articles.html',
                articles=queryset)
```

The `request` object has an attribute called `is_xhr` that you can check to see if the request is actually an Ajax request. Our preceding code will probably look better if we have it split into a few functions, such as a function to respond to Ajax requests and another to respond to plain HTTP requests. Why don't you try refactoring the code?

Our last example could also have a different approach; we could render the HTML template without adding context variables to it but by loading all of our data through Ajax requests. In this scenario, the following changes to the code would be required:

```python
from marshmallow import Schema, fields
class ArticleSchema(Schema):
    """
    Article dict serializer
    """
    url = fields.Method("article_url")
    def article_url(self, article):
        return article.url()

    class Meta:
        # which fields should be serialized?
        fields = ('id', 'title', 'content', 'url')

@app.route("/articles/", methods=["GET"])
@app.route("/articles/<article_id>", methods=["GET"])
def articles(article_id=None):
    if article_id:
        if request.is_xhr:
            article = Article.query.get(article_id)
            if article is None:
                return jsonify({"msgs": ["the article you're looking
for could not be found"]}), 404

            result = article_schema.dump(article)
            return jsonify({'article': result})
        else:
            return render_template('article.html')
    else:
        if request.is_xhr:
            queryset = Article.query.limit(10)
            # never return the whole set! As it would be very slow
            result = articles_schema.dump(queryset)

            # jsonify serializes our dict into a proper flask response
            return jsonify({"articles": result.data})
        else:
            return render_template('articles.html')
```

We added a new field `url` to our schema in order to access the path to the article page from within the JavaScript code, as we return a JSON document to the template, and not an SQLAlchemy object, and, therefore, cannot access the model methods.

The `articles.html` file will look like this:

```html
<!doctype html>
<html>
<head>
  <meta charset="UTF-8">
  <title>Articles</title>
</head>
<body>
<ul id="articles">
</ul>

<script type="text/javascript"
    src="https://code.jquery.com/jquery-2.1.3.min.js"></script>
<script type="text/javascript">
  // only execute after loading the whole HTML
  $(document).ready(function(){
    $.ajax({
      url:"{{ url_for('.articles') }}",
      success: function(data, textStatus, xhr){
        $(data['articles']).each(function(i, el){
          var link = "<a href='"+ el['url'] +"'>" + el['title'] +
            "</a>";
          $("#articles").append("<li>" + link + "</li>");
        });}});}); // don't do this in live code
</script>
</body>
</html>
```

In our template, our article list is empty; we then populate it after calling our service with Ajax. If you test the full example, the Ajax request is so fast you might not even notice the page was loaded empty before being populated with Ajax.

Beyond GET

So far we've had a few cozy examples with Ajax and RESTful Web services but we have yet to record data in our database using a service. How about trying that now?

Recording to the database using Web services is not much different from what we have done in the previous chapter. We'll receive data from an Ajax request, we will check which HTTP method was used in order to decide what to do, then we'll validate the sent data and save everything if no error was found. In *Chapter 4, Please Fill in This Form, Madam*, we talked about CSRF protection and its importance. We'll keep validating our data against CSRF with our Web service. The trick is to add the CSRF token to the form data being submitted. See the attached code provided with the eBook for the example HTML.

This is how our view looks like with POST, PUT, and REMOVE method support:

```python
@app.route("/articles/", methods=["GET", "POST"])
@app.route("/articles/<int:article_id>", methods=["GET", "PUT",
    "DELETE"])
def articles(article_id=None):
    if request.method == "GET":
        if article_id:
            article = Article.query.get(article_id)

            if request.is_xhr:
                if article is None:
                    return jsonify({"msgs": ["the article you're
                        looking for could not be found"]}), 404

                result = article_schema.dump(article)
                return jsonify({': result.data})

            return render_template('article.html',
                article=article, form=ArticleForm(obj=article))
        else:
            if request.is_xhr:
                # never return the whole set! As it would be very slow
                queryset = Article.query.limit(10)
                result = articles_schema.dump(queryset)

                # jsonify serializes our dict into a proper flask
response
                return jsonify({"articles": result.data})
    elif request.method == "POST" and request.is_xhr:
        form = ArticleForm(request.form)

        if form.validate():
            article = Article()
            form.populate_obj(article)
```

```
            db.session.add(article)
            db.session.commit()
            return jsonify({"msgs": ["article created"]})
        else:
            return jsonify({"msgs": ["the sent data is not
                valid"]}), 400

    elif request.method == "PUT" and request.is_xhr:
        article = Article.query.get(article_id)

        if article is None:
            return jsonify({"msgs": ["the article you're looking
                for could not be found"]}), 404

        form = ArticleForm(request.form, obj=article)

        if form.validate():
            form.populate_obj(article)
            db.session.add(article)
            db.session.commit()
            return jsonify({"msgs": ["article updated"]})
        else:
            return jsonify({"msgs": ["the sent data was not
                valid"]}), 400
    elif request.method == "DELETE" and request.is_xhr:
        article = Article.query.get(article_id)

        if article is None:
            return jsonify({"msgs": ["the article you're looking
                for could not be found"]}), 404

        db.session.delete(article)
        db.session.commit()
        return jsonify({"msgs": ["article removed"]})

    return render_template('articles.html', form=ArticleForm())
```

Ok, it's true, we can't hide it any longer; dealing with Web services and plain HTML rendering in the same page can be kind of messy, as seen in the preceding example. Even if you split the function between other functions, by method, things might not look that good. The usual pattern is to have a view serving your Ajax requests and another serving your "normal" requests. You only mix both of them if convenient.

Flask-Restless

Flask-Restless is an extension capable of auto-generating a whole RESTful API for your SQLAlchemy models with support for GET, POST, PUT, and DELETE. Most Web services won't need more than that. Another advantage to using Flask-Restless is the chance to extend the auto-generated methods with authentication validation, custom behavior, and custom queries. This is a must-learn extension!

Let's see how our Web service would look with Flask-Restless. We'll also have to install a new library for this example:

```
pip install Flask-Restless
```

And then:

```python
# coding:utf-8

from flask import Flask, url_for
from flask.ext.restless import APIManager
from flask.ext.sqlalchemy import SQLAlchemy

app = Flask(__name__)
app.config['SECRET_KEY'] = 'secret'
app.config['SQLALCHEMY_DATABASE_URI'] = \
    'sqlite:////tmp/employees.sqlite'

db = SQLAlchemy(app)


class Article(db.Model):
    __tablename__ = 'articles'

    id = db.Column(db.Integer, primary_key=True)
    title = db.Column(db.String(100), nullable=False)
    content = db.Column(db.String(255), nullable=False)

    def __unicode__(self):
        return self.content

    def url(self):
        return url_for('.articles', article_id=self.id)

# create the Flask-Restless API manager
manager = APIManager(app, flask_sqlalchemy_db=db)
```

```
# create our Article API at /api/articles
manager.create_api(Article, collection_name='articles',
methods=['GET', 'POST', 'PUT', 'DELETE'])

db.create_all()

if __name__ == '__main__':
    # we define the debug environment only if running through command
line
    app.config['SQLALCHEMY_ECHO'] = True
    app.debug = True
    app.run()
```

In the preceding example, we create our model, as before; then we create a
Flask-Restless API to hold all our model APIs; and then we create a Web service
API for `Article` with the prefix `articles` and support for the methods GET, POST,
PUT, and DELETE, each with the expected behavior: GET for consulting, POST for new
records, PUT for updates, and DELETE for deletes.

In your console, type the following command to send a GET request to the API and
test that your example is working:

`curl http://127.0.0.1:5000/api/articles`

As the Flask-Restless API is pretty extensive, we'll discuss briefly, a few common
options that come in handy for most projects.

The `serializer/deserializer` parameters for `create_api` are useful whenever
you need custom serialization/deserialization for your models. The usage is simple:

```
manager.create_api(Model, methods=METHODS,
                   serializer=my_serializer,
                   deserializer=my_deserializer)
def my_serializer(instance):
    return some_schema.dump(instance).data

def my_deserializer(data):
    return some_schema.load(data).data
```

You could use marshmallow to generate the schema, as in the preceding example.

Another useful set of options for `create_api` are `include_columns` and `exclude_columns`. They allow you to control how much data you want returned by your API and prevent sensitive data from being returned. When `include_columns` is set, only the fields defined in it are returned by GET requests. When `exclude_columns` is set, only the fields that are not defined in it are returned by GET requests. For example:

```
# both the statements below are equivalents
manager.create_api(Article, methods=['GET'],
    include_columns=['id', 'title'])
manager.create_api(Article, methods=['GET'],
    exclude_columns=['content'])
```

Summary

In this chapter, we learned what REST is, its advantages, how to create Flask RESTful Web Services and APIs, and how to use Flask-RESTless to make the whole thing work well. We also had an overview on what jQuery is and how to use it to send Ajax requests to consult our services. These chapter examples were pretty intense. Try to code the examples yourself, to assimilate them better.

In the next chapter, we'll be talking about the one way in which you can assure software quality: tests! We'll learn how to test our Web applications in the many ways that they may be tested and how to integrate these tests into our very coding routines. See you there!

7
If Ain't Tested,
It Ain't Game, Bro!

Does the software you write have quality? How do you attest that?

Software is usually written according to certain requested needs, be it bug reports, feature and enhancement tickets, or whatever. To have quality, the software must satisfy these needs wholly and precisely; that is, it should do what is expected of it.

Just as you would push a button to know what it does (given you do not have a manual), you have to test your code to know what it does or to attest what it should do. That's how you assure **software quality**.

During the course of a software development, it is usual to have many features that share some code base or library. You could, for example, change a piece of code to fix a bug and create another bug in another point in your code. Software tests also help with that as they assure that your code does what it should do; if you change a piece of broken code and break another piece of code, you'll also be breaking a test. In this scenario, if you make use of **continuous integration**, the broken code will never reach your production environment.

 Don't know what continuous integration is? Refer to `http://www.martinfowler.com/articles/continuousIntegration.html` and `https://jenkins-ci.org/`.

Tests are so important that there is a software development process called **Test Driven Development (TDD)**, which states that the test should be written before the actual code, and that the actual code is only *ready* when the test itself is satisfied. TDD is quite common among senior developers and beyond. Just for the fun of it, we'll be using TDD in this chapter, from top to toe.

What kinds of test are there?

We want tests, and we want them now; but what kind of test do we want?

There are two major classifications for tests, based on how much access to the internal code you have: **black-box** and **white-box** tests.

Black-box tests are where the testers do not have knowledge of, and/or access to, the actual code he/she is testing. In these cases, the test consists of checking whether the system states before and after the code execution are as expected or whether the given output corresponds to the given input.

White-box tests are a little different as you will have access to the actual code internals that you're testing as well as the system expected states before and after code execution and the expected output for a given input. This kind of test has a stronger subjective goal, usually related to performance and software quality.

In this chapter, we will cover how to implement black-box tests as they are more accessible to others and easier to implement. On the other hand, we'll overview the tools for executing white-box tests.

There are many ways a code base may be tested. We'll focus our efforts on two types of automated tests (we will not cover manual testing techniques), each with a different goal: **unit testing** and **behavior testing**. Each of these tests has a different purpose and complements the other. Let's take a look at what these tests are, when to use them, and how to run them with Flask.

Unit testing

Unit testing is a technique where you test the smallest piece of code that has meaningful functionality (called a **unit**) against an input and the expected output. You usually run unit tests against functions and methods in your code base that do not rely on other functions and methods that you've also written.

In a sense, testing is actually the art of stacking unit tests together (first test a function, then functions that interact with each other, then functions that interact with other systems) in a way that the whole system eventually becomes fully tested.

For unit testing with Python, we may use the `doctest` or `unittest` built-in modules. The `doctest` module is useful for running embedded interactive code examples from an object documentation as test cases. Doctests are a nice complement to Unittest, which is a more robust module focused on helping you write unit tests (as the name implies), and should, preferably, not be used alone. Let's see an example:

```python
# coding:utf-8

"""Doctest example"""

import doctest
import unittest


def sum_fnc(a, b):
    """
    Returns a + b

    >>> sum_fnc(10, 20)
    30
    >>> sum_fnc(-10, -20)
    -30
    >>> sum_fnc(10, -20)
    -10
    """
    return a + b


class TestSumFnc(unittest.TestCase):
    def test_sum_with_positive_numbers(self):
        result = sum_fnc(10, 20)
        self.assertEqual(result, 30)

    def test_sum_with_negative_numbers(self):
        result = sum_fnc(-10, -20)
        self.assertEqual(result, -30)

    def test_sum_with_mixed_signal_numbers(self):
        result = sum_fnc(10, -20)
        self.assertEqual(result, -10)


if __name__ == '__main__':
    doctest.testmod(verbose=1)
    unittest.main()
```

In the preceding example, we define a simple `sum_fnc` function, which receives two parameters and returns its sum. The `sum_fnc` function has a docstring explaining itself. In this docstring, we have an interactive code example of the function call and output. This code example is invoked by `doctest.testmod()`, which checks whether the given output is correct for the function called.

Next, we have a `TestCase` called `TestSumFnc`, which defines three test methods (`test_<test_name>`) and does almost exactly what our docstring test does. The difference of this approach is that we are capable of discovering what is wrong without the test result, *if* something is wrong. If we wished, for both our docstring and test case, to do exactly the same, we would have used the `assert` Python keyword to compare the result with the expected result in the test methods. Instead, we used the `assertEqual` method, which not only tells us that something is wrong with the result if something is wrong, but also informs us that the problem is that both the result and the expected values are not equal.

If we wished to check whether our result is, for example, larger than a certain value, we would have used the method `assertGreater` or `assertGreaterEqual` so that an assertion error would have also told us what kind of error we had.

> Good tests are independent from each other so that a failed test may never prevent another test from running. Importing the test dependencies from within the test and cleaning the database are common ways to do that.

The preceding case is common when writing scripts or desktop applications. A web application has different needs regarding the tests. A web application code usually runs in response to user interaction through a browser request and returns a response as the output. To test in this kind of environment, we have to simulate requests and properly test the response content, which is usually not as straightforward as the output of our `sum_fnc`. A response may be any kind of document and it may have different sizes and content, and you even have to worry about the response HTTP code, which holds a lot of contextual meaning.

To help you test your views and simulate user interaction with your web application, Flask gives you a test client tool through which you can send requests in any valid HTTP method to your application. For example, You may consult a service through a PUT request, or a regular view through GET. Here's an example:

```
# coding:utf-8

from flask import Flask, url_for, request
import unittest
```

```python
def setup_database(app):
    # setup database ...
    pass


def setup(app):
    from flask import request, render_template

    # this is not a good production setup
    # you should register blueprints here
    @app.route("/")
    def index_view():
        return render_template('index.html',
            name=request.args.get('name'))


def app_factory(name=__name__, debug=True):
    app = Flask(name)
    app.debug = debug
    setup_database(app)
    setup(app)
    return app


class TestWebApp(unittest.TestCase):
    def setUp(self):
        # setUp is called before each test method
        # we create a clean app for each test
        self.app = app_factory()
        # we create a clean client for each test
        self.client = self.app.test_client()

    def tearDown(self):
        # release resources here
        # usually, you clean or destroy the test database
        pass

    def test_index_no_arguments(self):
        with self.app.test_request_context():
            path = url_for('index_view')
            resp = self.client.get(path)
            # check response content
            self.assertIn('Hello World', resp.data)

    def test_index_with_name(self):
        with self.app.test_request_context():
            name = 'Amazing You'
```

```
path = url_for('index_view', name=name)
resp = self.client.get(path)
# check response content
self.assertIn(name, resp.data)


if __name__ == '__main__':
    unittest.main()
```

The preceding example is a complete one. We use the `app_factory` pattern to create our application, then we create an app and client inside `setUp`, which is run before every test method, and we create two tests, one for when the request receives a name parameter and another for when it doesn't. As we do not create any persistent resources, our `tearDown` method is empty. If we had we a database connection with fixtures of any kind, we would have to reset the database state inside `tearDown` or even drop the database.

Also, be aware of `test_request_context`, which is used to create a request context inside our tests. We create this context so that `url_for`, which requires a request context if `SERVER_NAME` config is not set, is able to return our view path.

 Set the `SERVER_NAME` config if your website uses a subdomain.

Behavior testing

In unit testing, we tested the output of functions against an expected result. If that result was not what we were waiting for, an assertion exception would be raised to notify a problem. It's a simple black-box test. Now, some weird questions: did you notice your test is written in a way different from how a bug report or feature request is written? Did you notice that your test cannot be read by nontech people because it is, actually, code?

I would like to introduce you to lettuce (`http://lettuce.it/`), a tool capable of converting the **Gherkin** language tests into actual tests.

 For an overview on the Gherkin language, visit `https://github.com/cucumber/cucumber/wiki/Gherkin`.

Lettuce helps you translate the actual user-written features into test method calls. This way, a feature request like:

Feature: compute sum

In order to compute a sum

As student

Implement sum_fnc

- **Scenario**: Sum of positives
    - ○ **Given** I have the numbers 10 and 20
    - ○ **When** I sum them
    - ○ **Then** I see the result 30

- **Scenario**: Sum of negatives
    - ○ **Given** I have the numbers -10 and -20
    - ○ **When** I sum them
    - ○ **Then** I see the result -30

- **Scenario**: Sum with mixed signals
    - ○ **Given** I have the numbers 10 and -20
    - ○ **When** I sum them
    - ○ **Then** I see the result -10

The feature could be translated into the actual code that will test our software. Make sure lettuce is properly installed:

```
pip install lettuce python-Levenshtein
```

Create a `features` directory and place a `steps.py` (or any other Python filename you like) there with the following code:

```python
# coding:utf-8
from lettuce import *
from lib import sum_fnc


@step('Given I have the numbers (\-?\d+) and (\-?\d+)')
def have_the_numbers(step, *numbers):
    numbers = map(lambda n: int(n), numbers)
    world.numbers = numbers

@step('When I sum them')
def compute_sum(step):
    world.result = sum_fnc(*world.numbers)

@step('Then I see the result (\-?\d+)')
```

```
def check_number(step, expected):
    expected = int(expected)
    assert world.result == expected, "Got %d; expected %d" %
        (world.result, expected)
```

What did we just do now? We defined three test functions, have_the_numbers, compute_sum and check_number, where each receives as first argument a `step` instance and other parameters for the actual test. The step decorator, used to decorate our functions, is used to map a string pattern parsed from our Gherkin text into the function itself. Another responsibility for our decorator is to parse the arguments mapped from the step argument to the function as a parameter.

For example, the step for `have_the_numbers` has a regular expression pattern (\-?\d+) and (\-?\d+), which maps two numbers to the `numbers` parameter of our function. These values are fetched from our Gherkin input text. For the given scenarios, these numbers would be [10, 20], [-10, -20], and [10, -20], respectively. At last, `world` is a global variable you may use to share values between the steps.

Using features to describe behavior is very healthy for the development process because it brings business people closer to what is being created, though it is quite verbose. Also, because it is verbose, its use is not advised for testing isolated functions as we did in our preceding example. As behavior should be written preferably by business people, it should also test behavior the person writing can visually attest. For example, "If I click on a button, I get the lowest price for something" or "Given I access a certain page, I see some message or some links".

"Click here, and something happens there". Checking rendered request responses is kind of tricky, if you ask me. Why? In our second example, we verify if a given string value is inside our `resp.data`, and that was OK because our response is returned `complete`. We do not use JavaScript to render anything after the page is loaded or to show messages. If this had been the case, our verification would have probably returned a wrong result because the JavaScript code would not have been executed.

To correctly render and verify a `view` response, we may use a headless browser such as **Selenium** or **PhantomJS** (refer to https://pythonhosted.org/Flask-Testing/#testing-with-liveserver). The **Flask-testing** extension will be of help too.

Flask-testing

Like most Flask extensions, Flask-testing does not do much, but what it does, it does beautifully! We will discuss some very useful features that Flask-testing gives you out of the box: LiveServer setup, extra assertions, and the JSON response handle. Make sure it is installed before continuing:

```
pip install flask-testing blinker
```

LiveServer

LiveServer is a Flask-testing tool that allows you to connect to headless browsers, a browser that do not render the content visually (such as Firefox or Chrome) but executes all scripts and styling and simulates user interaction. Use LiveServer whenever you need to evaluate the page content after JavaScript interaction. We'll use PhantomJS as our headless browser. My advice to you is that you install the old browser, like our ancestors did, compiling it from source. Follow these instructions at `http://phantomjs.org/build.html` (you may have to install a few extra libraries in order to get full functionality from phantom). The `build.sh` file will advise you to install it when necessary).

> After compiling **PhantomJS**, make sure it is found in by your PATH by moving the binary `bin/phantomjs` to `/usr/local/bin`.

Make sure Selenium is installed:

pip install selenium

And our code will look like this:

```
# coding:utf-8

"""
Example adapted from https://pythonhosted.org/Flask-Testing/#testing-
with-liveserver
"""

import urllib2
from urlparse import urljoin
from selenium import webdriver
from flask import Flask, render_template, jsonify, url_for
from flask.ext.testing import LiveServerTestCase
from random import choice


my_lines = ['Hello there!', 'How do you do?', 'Flask is great, ain't
it?']


def setup(app):
    @app.route("/")
    def index_view():
        return render_template('js_index.html')

    @app.route("/text")
```

```
        def text_view():
            return jsonify({'text': choice(my_lines)})


    def app_factory(name=None):
        name = name or __name__
        app = Flask(name)
        setup(app)
        return app


    class IndexTest(LiveServerTestCase):
        def setUp(self):
            self.driver = webdriver.PhantomJS()

        def tearDown(self):
            self.driver.close()

        def create_app(self):
            app = app_factory()
            app.config['TESTING'] = True
            # default port is 5000
            app.config['LIVESERVER_PORT'] = 8943
            return app

        def test_server_is_up_and_running(self):
            resp = urllib2.urlopen(self.get_server_url())
            self.assertEqual(resp.code, 200)

        def test_random_text_was_loaded(self):
            with self.app.test_request_context():
                domain = self.get_server_url()
                path = url_for('.index_view')
                url = urljoin(domain, path)

                self.driver.get(url)
                fillme_element =
                    self.driver.find_element_by_id('fillme')
                fillme_text = fillme_element.text
                self.assertIn(fillme_text, my_lines)


    if __name__ == '__main__':
        import unittest
        unittest.main()
```

The `templates/js_index.html` file should look like this:

```
<html>
<head><title>Hello You</title></head>
<body>
<span id="fillme"></span>

<!-- Loading JQuery from CDN -->
<!-- what's a CDN? http://www.rackspace.com/knowledge_center/article/
what-is-a-cdn --
    >
<script type="text/javascript" src="https://code.jquery.com/jquery-
2.1.3.min.js"></script>
<script type="text/javascript">
  $(document).ready(function(){
    $.getJSON("{{ url_for('.text_view') }}",
    function(data){
        $('#fillme').text(data['text']);
    });
  });
</script>
</body></html>
```

The preceding example is quite simple. We define our factory, which creates our app with the two views attached. One returns a `js_index.html` that has a script that consults our second view for a phrase and populates the `fillme` HTML element, and the second view returns a phrase in JSON format, chosen randomly from a predefined list.

We then define `IndexTest` that extends `LiveServerTestCase`, a special class we use to run our live server tests. We set our live server to run on a different port from the default, but that's not required.

Inside `setUp`, we create a `driver` with selenium WebDriver. The driver is something similar to a browser. We'll use it to access and inspect our application through the LiveServer. The `tearDown` makes sure our driver is closed after each test and resources are released.

`test_server_is_up_and_running` is self explanatory and not actually necessary in real-world tests.

Then we have `test_random_text_was_loaded`, which is a pretty busy test. We use `test_request_context` in order to create a request context to generate our URL paths with `url_open`. `get_server_url`, which will return us our live server URL; we join this with our view path and load it into our driver.

With the URL loaded (be aware that the URL was not only loaded, but the scripts were also executed), we use `find_element_by_id` to look for the element `fillme` and assert that its text context has one of the expected values. This is a simple example. You can, for example, test for whether a button is in the expected place; submit a form; and trigger a JavaScript function. Selenium plus PhantomJS is a powerful combination.

> When your development is driven by feature testing, you're actually not using **TDD**, but **Behavior Driven Development (BDD)**. A mix of both techniques is, usually, what you want.

Extra assertions

When testing your code, you'll notice a few tests are kind of repetitive. To handle this scenario, one would create a custom TestCases with specific routines and extend the tests accordingly. With Flask-testing, you still have to do that, but will have to code a little less to test your Flask views as `flask.ext.testing.TestCase` is bundled with common assertions, many found in frameworks such as Django. Let's see the most important (in my opinion, of course) assertions:

- `assert_context(name, value)`: This asserts that a variable is in the template context. Use it to verify that a given response context has the right values for a variable.

- `assert_redirects(response, location)`: This asserts that the response is a redirect and gives its location. It's a good practice to redirect after writing to storage, like after a successful POST, which is a good use case for this assertion.

- `assert_template_used(name, tmpl_name_attribute='name')`: This asserts that a given template is used in the request (`tmpl_name_attribute` is only needed if you're not using Jinja2; not in our case); use it whenever you render an HTML template, really!

- `assert404(response, message=None)`: This asserts that the response has the 404 HTTP code; it is useful for "rainy day" scenarios; that is, when someone is trying to access something that does not exist. It is very useful.

JSON handle

Here is a lovely trick Flask-testing has for you. Whenever you return a JSON response from your views, your response will have an extra attribute called `json`. That's your JSON-converted response! Here is an example:

```
# example from https://pythonhosted.org/Flask-Testing/#testing-json-
responses
@app.route("/ajax/")
```

```
def some_json():
    return jsonify(success=True)

class TestViews(TestCase):
    def test_some_json(self):
        response = self.client.get("/ajax/")
        self.assertEquals(response.json, dict(success=True))
```

Fixtures

Good tests are always executed considering a predefined, reproducible application state; that is, whenever you run a test in the chosen state, the result will always be equivalent. Usually, this is achieved by setting your database data yourself and clearing your cache and any temporary files (if you make use of external services, you should mock them) for each test. Clearing cache and temporary files is not hard, while setting your database data, on the other hand, is.

If you're using **Flask-SQLAlchemy** to hold your data, you would need to hardcode, somewhere in your tests as follows:

```
attributes = { ... }
model = MyModel(**attributes)
db.session.add(model)
db.session.commit()
```

This approach does not scale as it is not easily reusable (when you define this as a function and a method, define it for each test). There are two ways to populate your database for testing: **fixtures** and **pseudo-random data**.

Using pseudo-random data is usually library-specific and produces better test data as the generated data is context-specific, not static, but it may require specific coding now and then, just like when you define your own fields or need a different value range for a field.

Fixtures are the most straightforward way as you just have to define your data in a file and load it at each test. You can do that by exporting your database data, editing at your convenience, or writing it yourself. The JSON format is quite popular for this. Let's take a look on how to implement both:

```
# coding:utf-8
# == USING FIXTURES ===
import tempfile, os
import json

from flask import Flask
```

```
from flask.ext.testing import TestCase
from flask.ext.sqlalchemy import SQLAlchemy


db = SQLAlchemy()


class User(db.Model):
    id = db.Column(db.Integer, primary_key=True)
    name = db.Column(db.String(255))
    gender = db.Column(db.String(1), default='U')

    def __unicode__(self):
        return self.name


def app_factory(name=None):
    name = name or __name__
    app = Flask(name)
    return app


class MyTestCase(TestCase):
    def create_app(self):
        app = app_factory()
        app.config['TESTING'] = True
        # db_fd: database file descriptor
        # we create a temporary file to hold our data
        self.db_fd, app.config['DATABASE'] = tempfile.mkstemp()
        db.init_app(app)
        return app

    def load_fixture(self, path, model_cls):
        """
        Loads a json fixture into the database
        """
        fixture = json.load(open(path))

        for data in fixture:
            # Model accepts dict like parameter
            instance = model_cls(**data)
            # makes sure our session knows about our new instance
            db.session.add(instance)
```

```
                db.session.commit()

        def setUp(self):
            db.create_all()
            # you could load more fixtures if needed
            self.load_fixture('fixtures/users.json', User)

        def tearDown(self):
            # makes sure the session is removed
            db.session.remove()

            # close file descriptor
            os.close(self.db_fd)

            # delete temporary database file
            # as SQLite database is a single file, this is equivalent to a
    drop_all
            os.unlink(self.app.config['DATABASE'])

        def test_fixture(self):
            marie =
                User.query.filter(User.name.ilike('Marie%')).first()
            self.assertEqual(marie.gender, "F")

    if __name__ == '__main__':
        import unittest
        unittest.main()
```

The preceding code is simple. We create a SQLAlchemy model, link it to our app, and, during the setup, we load our fixture. In tearDown, we make sure our database and SQLAlchemy session are brand new for the next test. Our fixture is written using JSON format because it is fast enough and readable.

Were we to use pseudo-random generators to create our users, (look up Google **fuzzy testing** for more on the subject), we could do it like this:

```
def new_user(**kw):
    # this way we only know the user data in execution time
    # tests should consider it
    kw['name'] = kw.get('name', "%s %s" % (choice(names),
        choice(surnames)) )
    kw['gender'] = kw.get('gender', choice(['M', 'F', 'U']))
    return kw
user = User(**new_user())
db.session.add(user)
db.session.commit()
```

Be aware that our tests would also have to change as we are not testing against a static scenario. As a rule, fixtures will be enough in most cases, but pseudo-random test data is better in most cases as it forces your application to handle real scenarios, which are, usually left out.

Extra – integration testing

Integration testing is a very widely used term/concept with a very narrow meaning. It is used to refer to the act of testing multiple modules together to test their integration. As testing multiple modules together from the same code base with Python is usually trivial and transparent (an import here, a call there, and some output checking), you'll usually hear people using the term **integration testing** while referring to testing their code against a different code base, an application they did not create or maintain, or when a new key functionality was added to the system.

Summary

Whoa! We just survived a chapter about testing software! That's something to be proud of. We learned a few concepts such as TDD, white-box, and black-box testing. We also learned how to create unit tests; test our views; write features using the Gherkin language and test them using lettuce; use Flask-testing, Selenium with PhantomJS to test a HTML response from the user perspective; also how to use fixtures to control our application state for proper reproducible testing. Now you are capable of testing Flask applications in different ways using the correct techniques for different scenarios and needs.

In the next chapter, things are gonna go wild really fast as our subject of study will be tricks with Flask. Blueprints, sessions, logging, debugging, and so on, will be covered in the next chapter, allowing you to create even more robust software. See you there!

8

Tips and Tricks or Flask Wizardry 101

Can you wait any longer before trying more advanced topics on Flask? I certainly can't! In this chapter, we'll study techniques and modules essential to work better and more efficiently with Flask.

What good is high-quality software that takes forever to code or low-quality software delivered in a jiffy? Real Web development, the one you get paid for at the end of the month, requires maintainability, productivity, and quality to be feasible.

As we discussed earlier, software quality is closely related to testing. One way to measure software quality is verifying how close its features are to what is expected of it. This kind of measuring does not take into account the subjective side of quality evaluation. A client, per example, may believe the design of his latest project is ugly and consider a well tested, feature-adherent Web project *crappy*. The most you can do in these cases is charge a few extra bucks for a design refactory.

 Bring your client closer to the development process in order to avoid this kind of situation, if it ever happens to you. Try searching for "scrum" in Google or DuckDuckGo.

When talking about **productivity** and **maintainability**, the approaches are many! You may purchase a nice Integrated Development Environment (IDE) such as PyCharm or WingIDE to improve your productivity or hire third-party services to help you test your code or control your development schedule, but these can do just so much. Good architecture and task automation will be your best friend in most projects. Before discussing suggestions on how to organize you code and which modules will help you save some typing here and there, let's discuss premature optimization and overengineering, two terrible symptoms of an anxious developer/analyst/nosy manager.

Overengineering

Making software is like making a condo, in a few ways. You'll plan ahead what you want to create before starting so that waste is kept to a minimum. Contrary to a condo, where it's advisable to plan the whole project before you start, you do not have to plan out your software because it will most likely change during development, and a lot of the planning may just go to waste.

The problem with this "plan just enough" approach is that you don't know what to expect in the future, which may transform the little bit of paranoia we all have inside into something big. One may end up coding against total system failure or complex software requirement scenarios that may never happen. You don't need a multilayer architecture, with cache, database integration, signaling system, and so on, to create a hello world, nor do you need less than this to create a Facebook clone.

The message here is: do not make your product more robust or complex than you know it needs to be and do not waste time planning for what may, most likely, never happen.

 Always plan for reasonable levels of safety, complexity, and performance.

Premature optimization

Is your software fast enough? Don't know? Then why are you optimizing that code, my friend? When you spend time optimizing software that you're not sure needs optimization, if no one complained about it being slow or you do not notice it to be slow in daily use, you're probably wasting time with premature optimization.

And so, on to Flask.

Blueprints 101

So far, our applications have all been flat: beautiful, single-file Web applications (templates and static resources not considered). In some cases, that's a nice approach; a reduced need for imports, easy to maintain with simple editors and all but…

As our applications grow, we identify the need to contextually arrange our code. Flask Blueprints allow you to modularize your project, sharding your views in "app-like" objects called **blueprints** that can be later loaded and exposed by your Flask application. Large applications benefit deeply from the use of blueprints, as the code gets more organized.

Feature-wise, it also helps you configure the registered view access and resource lookup in a more monolithic way. Tests, models, templates and static resources can be sorted by blueprint, making your code so much more maintainable. If you're familiar with **Django**, think of blueprints as Django apps. This way, a registered blueprint has access to the application config and may be registered with different routes.

Unlike Django apps, blueprints do not enforce a specific structure, just like the Flask application itself. You may have a blueprint structured as a module, for example, which is kind of convenient, once in a while.

An example always helps, right? Let's see a good example of blueprints. First, we installed the required library for the example in our virtual environment:

```
# library for parsing and reading our HTML
pip install lxml
# our test-friendly library
pip install flask-testing
```

And then we defined our tests (because we love TDD!):

```
# coding:utf-8
# runtests.py

import lxml.html

from flask.ext.testing import TestCase
from flask import url_for
from main import app_factory
from database import db


class BaseTest(object):
    """
    Base test case. Our test cases should extend this class.
    It handles database creation and clean up.
    """

    def create_app(self):
        app = app_factory()
        app.config['TESTING'] = True
        return app

    def setUp(self):
        self.app.config['SQLALCHEMY_DATABASE_URI'] =
            'sqlite:////tmp/ex01_test.sqlite'
        db.create_all()
```

```
    def tearDown(self):
        db.session.remove()
        db.drop_all()


class PostDetailTest(BaseTest, TestCase):
    def add_single_post(self):
        from blog import Post

        db.session.add(Post(title='Some text', slug='some-text',
            content='some content'))
        db.session.commit()

        assert Post.query.count() == 1

    def setUp(self):
        super(PostDetailTest, self).setUp()
        self.add_single_post()

    def test_get_request(self):
        with self.app.test_request_context():
            url = url_for('blog.posts_view', slug='some-text')
            resp = self.client.get(url)
            self.assert200(resp)
            self.assertTemplateUsed('post.html')
            self.assertIn('Some text', resp.data)


class PostListTest(BaseTest, TestCase):
    def add_posts(self):
        from blog import Post

        db.session.add_all([
            Post(title='Some text', slug='some-text',
                content='some content'),
            Post(title='Some more text', slug='some-more-text',
                content='some more content'),
            Post(title='Here we go', slug='here-we-go',
                content='here we go!'),
        ])
        db.session.commit()

        assert Post.query.count() == 3

    def add_multiple_posts(self, count):
        from blog import Post
```

```
        db.session.add_all([
            Post(title='%d' % i, slug='%d' % i, content='content
                %d' % i) for i in range(count)
        ])
        db.session.commit()

        assert Post.query.count() == count

    def test_get_posts(self):
        self.add_posts()

        # as we want to use url_for ...
        with self.app.test_request_context():
            url = url_for('blog.posts_view')
            resp = self.client.get(url)

            self.assert200(resp)
            self.assertIn('Some text', resp.data)
            self.assertIn('Some more text', resp.data)
            self.assertIn('Here we go', resp.data)
            self.assertTemplateUsed('posts.html')

    def test_page_number(self):
        self.add_multiple_posts(15)

        with self.app.test_request_context():
            url = url_for('blog.posts_view')
            resp = self.client.get(url)

            self.assert200(resp)

            # we use lxml to count how many li results were returned
            handle = lxml.html.fromstring(resp.data)
            self.assertEqual(10, len(handle.xpath("//ul/li")))


if __name__ == '__main__':
    import unittest
    unittest.main()
```

In the preceding code, we test a single view, blog.posts_view, that has two routes, one for post detail and another for post listing. If our view receives a slug parameter, it should return only the first Post that has the attribute value of slug; if not, it returns up to 10 results.

We may now create a view, using blueprints that satisfy our tests:

```python
# coding:utf-8
# blog.py

from flask import Blueprint, render_template, request
from database import db


# app is usually a good name for your blueprint instance
app = Blueprint(
    'blog',  # our blueprint name and endpoint prefix
    # template_folder points out to a templates folder in the current
module directory
    __name__, template_folder='templates'
)


class Post(db.Model):
    __tablename__ = 'posts'

    id = db.Column(db.Integer, primary_key=True)
    title = db.Column(db.String(100), nullable=False)
    slug = db.Column(db.String(100), nullable=False, unique=True)
    content = db.Column(db.Text(), nullable=False)

    def __unicode__(self):
        return self.title


@app.route("/")
@app.route("/<slug>")
def posts_view(slug=None):
    if slug is not None:
        post = Post.query.filter_by(slug=slug).first()
        return render_template('post.html', post=post)

    # lets paginate our result
    page_number = into(request.args.get('page', 1))
    page = Post.query.paginate(page_number, 10)

    return render_template('posts.html', page=page)
```

Creating a blueprint is pretty simple: we provide the blueprint name, which is also used as an endpoint prefix to all the blueprint views, the import name (usually __name__), and any extra arguments we see fit. In the example, we pass template_folder as the argument because we want to make use of templates. If you were coding a service, you could skip this parameter. Another very useful parameter is url_prefix, which allows us to define a default URL prefix for all our paths.

 If our blueprint name is blog and we register a method index_view, our endpoint to that view will be blog. index_view. An endpoint is a "name reference" to your view you may translate into its URL path.

The next step is to register our blueprint to our Flask application in order to make the views we wrote accessible. A database.py module is also created to hold our db instance.

Be warned that our Post model will be recognized by db.create_all because it was defined in blog.py; thus it becomes visible when the module is imported.

 If you have a model class defined in a module that is not imported anywhere, its tables may not be created because SQLAlchemy will not know of it. One way to avoid this situation is to have all your models imported by the module where the blueprint is defined.

```
# coding:utf-8
# database.py
from flask.ext.sqlalchemy import SQLAlchemy

db = SQLAlchemy()
## database.py END


# coding:utf-8
# main.py
from flask import Flask
from database import db
from blog import app as blog_bp


def app_factory(name=None):
    app = Flask(name or __name__)
    app.config['SQLALCHEMY_DATABASE_URI'] =
        'sqlite:////tmp/ex01.db'
```

```
db.init_app(app)

# let Flask know about blog blueprint
app.register_blueprint(blog_bp)
return app


# running or importing?
if __name__ == '__main__':
    app = app_factory()
    app.debug = True

    # make sure our tables are created
    with app.test_request_context():
        db.create_all()

    app.run()
```

What have we here? An `app_factory` that creates our Flask application sets the default database in `/tmp/`, a common Linux folder for temporary files; initiates our database manager, defined in `database.py`; and registers our blueprint using `register_blueprint`.

We set a routine to verify if we're running or importing the given module (useful for `runtests.py` as it imports from `main.py`); if we're running it, we create an app, set it to debug mode (because we're developing), create the database inside a temporary test context (`create_all` will not run outside a context), and run the app.

The templates (`post.html` and `posts.html`) still need to be written. Can you write them in order to make the tests pass? I leave it as a job for you!

Our current example project structure should look like this:

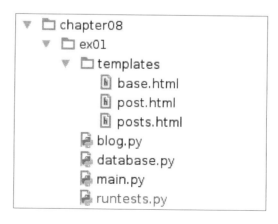

Well, our project is still flat; all modules on the same level, contextually arranged, but flat. Let's try moving our blog blueprint into its own module! We probably want something like this:

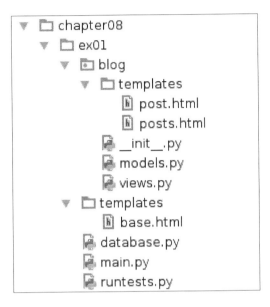

Blog templates inside a templates folder inside the blog package, our models inside `models.py`, and our views inside `views.py` (much like a Django app, right?).

It's possible to make that change without much effort. Mostly, create a `blog` folder and put an __init__.py file with the following content inside:

```
# coding:utf-8
from views import *
```

Move the `Post` class definition and db import into `models.py` and move blog-specific templates, `post.html` and `posts.html`, into a `templates` folder inside the package. As `template_folder` is relative to the current module directory, there is no need to change our blueprint instantiation. Now, run your tests. They should work without modification.

Take a sip, put on your war helmet, and let's move on to the next topic: logging!

Oh God, please tell me you have the logs...

You never know how much logging is important until you face a mysterious problem you can't quite figure out. Understanding why something wrong happened is the first, and probably main, reason why people add logging to their projects. But, hey, what's logging?

Logging is the act of storing records about events for further later analysis. An important concept about logging is related to the logging level, which allows you to categorize the information type and relevance.

The Python standard library comes bundled with a logging library that is actually pretty powerful and allows you, through handlers and messages, to log to streams, files, e-mail, or any other solution you believe will fit. Let's try a few useful logging examples, shall we?

```
# coding:utf-8
from flask import Flask
import logging
from logging.handlers import RotatingFileHandler


app = Flask(__name__)


# default flask logging handler pushes messages into the console
# works DEBUG mode only
app.config['LOG_FILENAME'] = '/var/tmp/project_name.log'
# log warning messages or higher
app.config['LOG_LEVEL'] = logging.WARNING
app.config['ADMINS'] = ['you@domain.com']
app.config['ENV'] = 'production'


def configure_file_logger(app, filename, level=logging.DEBUG):
    # special file handler that overwrites logging file after
    file_handler = RotatingFileHandler(
        filename=filename,
        encoding='utf-8',  # cool kids use utf-8
        maxBytes=1024 * 1024 * 32,  # we don't want super huge log
            files ...
        backupCount=3  # keep up to 3 old log files before rolling
            over
    )

    # define how our log messages should look like
```

```
    formatter = logging.Formatter(u"%(asctime)s %(levelname)s\t:
        %(message)s")
    file_handler.setFormatter(formatter)
    file_handler.setLevel(level)

    app.logger.addHandler(file_handler)


def configure_mail_logger(app, level=logging.ERROR):
    """
    Notify admins by e-mail in case of error for immediate action
    based on from http://flask.pocoo.org/docs/0.10/
errorhandling/#error-mails
    """

    if app.config['ENV'] == 'production':
        from logging.handlers import SMTPHandler

        mail_handler = SMTPHandler(
            '127.0.0.1',
            'server-error@domain.com',
            app.config['ADMINS'], 'YourApplication Failed')

        mail_handler.setLevel(level)
        app.logger.addHandler(mail_handler)


if __name__ == '__main__':
    app.debug = True
    configure_file_logger(app, '/var/tmp/project_name.dev.log')
    configure_mail_logger(app)
    app.run()
```

In our example, we create two common logging setups: logging to a file and logging to mail. Both are very useful in their own way. In `configure_file_logger` we define a function that registers a `RotatingFileHandler` to hold all log messages with the given level or above. Here, we do not use a regular `FileHandler` class because we want to keep our log files manageable (also known as: small). `RotatingFileHandler` allows us to define a max size for our log files and, when the log file size is close to the `maxBytes` limit, the handler "rotates" to a brand new log file (or overwrites an old one).

Logging to file is pretty straightforward and is used mostly to follow execution flows in applications (INFO, DEBUG, and WARN logs, mostly). Basically, file logging should be used whenever you have messages that should be recorded but should not be immediately read or even read at all (you might want to read a DEBUG log if something unexpected happens, but not otherwise). That way, in the case of a problem, you just dig out your log files and see what went wrong. Mail logging has another goal ...

To configure our mail logger, we define a function called `configure_mail_logger`. It creates and registers a `SMTPHandler` to our logger at the given log level; that way, whenever a message with that log level or higher is logged, an e-mail message is sent to the registered ADMINS.

Mail logging has one main purpose: to notify someone (or a lot of people) ASAP that something important has happened, such as an error that may compromise the application. You probably don't want a logging level below ERROR set for this kind of handler, as there would be just too many mails to keep up with.

As a last piece of advice on logging, sane projects have good logging. It's usual to trace back a user issue report or even a mailed error message. Define good logging policies and follow them, build tools to analyze your logs, and set logging rotation parameters appropriate to the project needs. Projects that produce a lot of logging may need larger files while projects that do not have much logging could live well with a high value of `backupCount`. Always give it some thought.

Debugging, DebugToolbar, and happiness

When running your Flask project in debug mode (`app.debug = True`), whenever Flask detects that your code has changed it will restart your application. If the given change breaks your application, Flask will display an error message in the console that is actually very simple to analyze. You start reading from the bottom up until you find the first line that mentions a file you wrote; that's where the error was generated. Now, read from the top down until you find a line telling you exactly what the error was. If this approach is not sufficient and if you need to read a variable value—for example, to better understand what is going on—you may use `pdb`, the standard Python debugging library, like this:

```
# coding:utf-8
from flask import Flask

app = Flask(__name__)
```

```
@app.route("/")
def index_view(arg=None):
    import pdb; pdb.set_trace()  # @TODO remove me before commit
    return 'Arg is %s' % arg


if __name__ == '__main__':
    app.debug = True
    app.run()
```

Whenever `pdb.set_trace` is called, a `pdb` console, which is much like a Python console, will be opened. Thus you may consult the value of any values you need or even make code evaluations.

Using `pdb` is nice but, if you just want to keep up with what is happening with your requests—for example, the template used, CPU time (this can catch you out!), logged messages, and so on—Flask-DebugToolbar may be a very handy extension at your disposal.

Flask-DebugToolbar

Imagine you could see the CPU time of your requests directly in your rendered template, and may be verify which template was used to render that page or even edit it on-the-fly. Would that be nice? Would you like to see it come true? Then try the following example:

First, make sure the extension is installed:

pip install flask-debugtoolbar

And on to some fine code:

```
# coding:utf-8
from flask import Flask, render_template
from flask_debugtoolbar import DebugToolbarExtension

app = Flask(__name__)
# configure your application before initializing any extensions
app.debug = True
app.config['SECRET_KEY'] = 'secret'  # required for session cookies to
work
app.config['DEBUG_TB_TEMPLATE_EDITOR_ENABLED'] = True
toolbar = DebugToolbarExtension(app)


@app.route("/")
```

```
def index_view():
    # please, make sure templates/index.html exists ; )
    return render_template('index.html')


if __name__ == '__main__':
    app.run()
```

Using Flask-DebugToolbar has no mysteries. Set `debug` to `True`, add a `secret_key`, and initialize the extension. When you open `http://127.0.0.1:5000/` in your browser, you should see something like this:

The collapsible panel on the right is a bit of HTML the debug toolbar inserts in each HTML response that allows you to introspect your response without the need to use a debugger such as `pdb`. In the example, we set `DEBUG_TB_TEMPLATE_EDITOR_ENABLED` to `True`; this option tells DebugToolbar we wish to edit the rendered template right from the browser. Just navigate to **Templates | Edit Templates** to try it out.

Sessions or storing user data between requests

Sometimes you'll have a scenario in your application where data has to be kept between requests, but there is no need to persist it in the database, like an authentication token that identifies a logged user or which items a user added to his shopping cart. At those times of peril, use Flask sessions.

Flask sessions are a solution for transient storage between requests implemented using browser cookies and cryptography. Flask uses the secret key value to encrypt any values you set in the session before setting it in the cookies; this way, even if a malicious person has access to the victim's browser, it won't be possible to read the cookie's content.

> Because the secret key is used to encrypt the session data, it is important to have a strong value for your secret key. `os.urandom(24)` will likely create a strong secret key for the deploy environment.

The data stored in the session is transient because there is no guarantee it will be there at any time, as the user may clean the browser cookies or the cookie might just expire, but it will most likely be there if you set it. Always take that piece of information into account while developing.

One big advantage of a Flask session is its simplicity; you use it as if it was a regular dictionary, like this:

```
# coding:utf-8

from flask import Flask, render_template, session, flash
from flask.ext.sqlalchemy import SQLAlchemy


app = Flask(__name__)
# strong secret key!!
app.config['SECRET_KEY'] = '\xa6\xb5\x0e\x7f\xd3}\x0b-\xaa\x03\x03\
x82\x10\xbe\x1e0u\x93,{\xd4Z\xa3\x8f'
app.config['SQLALCHEMY_DATABASE_URI'] =
    'sqlite:////tmp/ex05.sqlite'
db = SQLAlchemy(app)


class Product(db.Model):
    __tablename__ = 'products'
```

```
        id = db.Column(db.Integer, primary_key=True)
        sku = db.Column(db.String(30), unique=True)
        name = db.Column(db.String(255), nullable=False)

        def __unicode__(self):
            return self.name


    @app.route("/cart/add/<sku>")
    def add_to_cart_view(sku):
        product = Product.query.filter_by(sku=sku).first()

        if product is not None:
            session['cart'] = session.get('cart') or dict()
            item = session['cart'].get(product.sku) or dict()
            item['qty'] = item.get('qty', 0) + 1
            session['cart'][product.sku] = item
            flash(u'%s add to cart. Total: %d' % (product,
                item['qty']))

        return render_template('cart.html')


    def init():
        """
        Initializes and populates the database
        """
        db.create_all()

        if Product.query.count() == 0:
            db.session.add_all([
                Product(sku='010', name='Boots'),
                Product(sku='020', name='Gauntlets'),
                Product(sku='030', name='Helmets'),
            ])
            db.session.commit()


if __name__ == '__main__':
    app.debug = True

    with app.test_request_context():
        init()

    app.run()
# == END
# cart.html
```

```
<html><head>
  <title>Cart</title>
</head><body>
{% with messages = get_flashed_messages() %}
  {% if messages %}
  <ul>
    {% for message in messages %}
    <li>{{ message }}</li>
    {% endfor %}
  {% endif %}
  </ul>
{% endwith %}
</body></html>
```

In the example, we define a very simple Product model, with ID, name, a sku
(a special field used to identify a product in a store), and a view that adds the
requested product to a cart in the user session. As you can see, we make no
assumption that there is any data in the session, always playing it safe. We also do not
need to "save" the session after changing it, because Flask is smart enough to notice
your session was changed and saves it auto-magically… Actually, there is a catch
here. Flask sessions can only detect the session was modified if you modify its first
level values. Example:

```
session['cart'] = dict()  # new cart
# modified tells me if session knows it was changed
assert session.modified == True
session.modified = False  # we force it to think it was not meddled
with
session['cart']['item'] = dict()
# session does not know that one of its children was modified
assert session.modified == False
# we tell it, forcing a update
session.modified =True
# session will be saved, now
```

Now run your project and open the URL http://localhost:5000/cart/add/010
in your browser. See how the counter goes up each time you reload? Well, that's the
session working!

Exercise

How about putting our knowledge to work? Try making a shop web application,
such as an online pet shop. It should have pet services, for example bathing and vet
consultations, and also a small store with pet accessories. It should be easy enough
(lots of work! but easy).

Summary

This was a dense chapter. We overviewed important concepts—such as performance and maintainability, productivity, and quality—had a quick discussion about premature optimization and overengineering, and focused our efforts on learning how to write better code with Flask.

Blueprints, which allow you to create robust large projects with Flask, were discussed with a full-range example; we learned about logging to file and mail and the importance of each, had a lovely time with Flask-DebugToolbar (so handy!) and took the default session setup and usage to heart.

You're now a capable Flask developer. I'm so proud!

As one first learns to drive before trying out drifting, we will begin our Flask drifting next chapter. Our focus will be on using the wide extension ecosystem available to Flask in order to create amazing projects. It will be lots of fun! See you there!

Extensions, How I Love Thee

We have been using extensions to amplify our examples for a few chapters now; Flask-SQLAlchemy was used to connect to a relational database, Flask-MongoEngine to connect to MongoDB, Flask-WTF to create flexible reusable forms, and so on. Extensions are a great way to add functionality to your projects without adding anything *in the way* of your code and, if you like what we've done so far, you're going to love this chapter because it is dedicated to extensions!

In this chapter, we'll learn about a few very popular extensions we have neglected so far. Shall we begin?

How to configure extensions

Flask extensions are modules you import, (usually) initialize, and use to integrate with third-party libraries. They're (also) usually imported from `flask.ext.<extension_name>` (which is part of the extension pattern) and should be available in the PyPi repository under the BSD, MIT, or another less restrictive license.

It's good practice for an extension to have two states: uninitialized and initialized. This is good practice because your Flask application may not be available at the time you instantiate your extension. Our example in the previous chapter only initializes Flask-SQLAlchemy after it is imported in the main module. Ok, nice to know but how is the initialization process important?

Well, it's through the initialization that the extension fetches its configuration from the application. For example:

```
from flask import Flask
import logging

# set configuration for your Flask application or extensions
class Config(object):
```

```
        LOG_LEVEL = logging.WARNING

    app = Flask(__name__)
    app.config.from_object(Config)
    app.run()
```

In the previous code, we create a configuration class and loaded it with `config.from_object`. This way, `LOG_LEVEL` became available to all extensions with a hold on the app instance through:

```
    app.config['LOG_LEVEL']
```

Another way to load a configuration into `app.config` is using environment variables. This approach is especially useful in deployment environments, because you don't want to store a sensitive deployment configuration in your version control repository (it's unsafe!). It works like this:

```
    ...
    app.config.from_envvar('PATH_TO_CONFIGURATION')
```

If `PATH_TO_CONFIGURATION` is set to a Python file path such as `/home/youruser/someconfig.py` then `someconfig.py` will be loaded into config. Do it like this:

 # in the console

export PATH_TO_CONFIGURATION=/home/youruser/someconfig.py

Then create the configuration:

```
    # someconfig.py
    import logging
    LOG_LEVEL = logging.WARNING
```

Both the earlier configuration schemes have the same result.

> Be warned that `from_envvar` will load the environment variable from the user running the project. If you export the environment variable to your user and run your project as another, like www-data, it may not be able to find your configuration.

Flask-Principal and Flask-Login (aka Batman and Robin)

As described in the project page (`https://pythonhosted.org/Flask-Principal/`), Flask-Principal is a permission extension. It manages who can access what and to what extent. You usually should use it with an authentication and session manager, as is the case of Flask-Login, another extension we'll learn in this section.

Flask-Principal handles permissions through four simple entities: **Identity**, **IdentityContext**, **Need**, and **Permission**.

- **Identity**: This implies the way Flask-Principal identifies a user.

- **IdentityContext**: This implies the context of a user tested against Permission. It is used to verify whether the user has the right to do something. It can be used as a decorator (block unauthorized access) or as a context manager (only execute).

  A **Need** is a criterion you need (aha moment!) to satisfy in order to do something, such as having a role or a permission. There are a few preset needs available with Principal, but you may create your own easily, as a Need is just a named tuple such as this one:

  ```
  from collections import namedtuple
    namedtuple('RoleNeed', ['role', 'admin'])
  ```

- **Permission**: This is a group of needs that should be satisfied in order to allow something. Interpret it as a guardian of resources.

Given that we have our authorization extension all set, we need to authorize against something. A usual scenario is to restrict access to an administrative interface to administrators (don't say anything). To do that, we need to identify who is an administrator and who isn't. Flask-Login can be of help here by providing us with user session management (login and logout). Let's try an example. First, we make sure the required dependencies are installed:

```
pip install flask-wtf flask-login flask-principal flask-sqlalchemy
```

And then:

```
# coding:utf-8
# this example is based in the examples available in flask-login and
flask-principal docs

from flask_wtf import Form

from wtforms import StringField, PasswordField, ValidationError
```

```
from wtforms import validators

from flask import Flask, flash, render_template, redirect, url_for,
request, session, current_app
from flask.ext.login import UserMixin
from flask.ext.sqlalchemy import SQLAlchemy
from flask.ext.login import LoginManager, login_user, logout_user,
    login_required, current_user
from flask.ext.principal import Principal, Permission, Identity,
    AnonymousIdentity, identity_changed
from flask.ext.principal import RoleNeed, UserNeed, identity_loaded


principal = Principal()
login_manager = LoginManager()
login_manager.login_view = 'login_view'
# you may also overwrite the default flashed login message
# login_manager.login_message = 'Please log in to access this page.'
db = SQLAlchemy()

# Create a permission with a single Need
# we use it to see if an user has the correct rights to do something
admin_permission = Permission(RoleNeed('admin'))
```

As our example now is just too big, we'll understand it piecemeal. First, we make the necessary imports and create our extension instances. We set the `login_view` for the `login_manager` so that it knows where to redirect our user if he tries to access a page that requires user authentication. Be aware that Flask-Principal does not handle or keep track of logged users. That is Flask-Login abracadabra!

We also create our `admin_permission`. Our admin permission has only one need: the role admin. This way, we are defining that, for our permission to accept a user, this user needs to have the Role `admin`.

```
# UserMixin implements some of the methods required by Flask-Login
class User(db.Model, UserMixin):
    __tablename__ = 'users'

    id = db.Column(db.Integer, primary_key=True)
    active = db.Column(db.Boolean, default=False)
    username = db.Column(db.String(60), unique=True,
        nullable=False)
    password = db.Column(db.String(20), nullable=False)
    roles = db.relationship(
        'Role', backref='roles', lazy='dynamic')
```

```python
def __unicode__(self):
    return self.username

# flask login expects an is_active method in your user model
# you usually inactivate a user account if you don't want it
# to have access to the system anymore
def is_active(self):
    """
    Tells flask-login if the user account is active
    """
    return self.active


class Role(db.Model):
    """
    Holds our user roles
    """
    __tablename__ = 'roles'
    name = db.Column(db.String(60), primary_key=True)
    user_id = db.Column(db.Integer, db.ForeignKey('users.id'))

    def __unicode__(self):
        return self.name
```

We have two models here, one to hold our user information and another to hold our user roles. A role is usually used to categorize users, like admin; you may have three admins in your system and all of them will have the role admin. As a result, they will all be able to do "admin stuff", if the permissions are properly configured. Notice we define an is_active method for User. That method is required and I advise you to always overwrite it, even though UserMixin already provides an implementation. is_active is used to tell login whether the user is active or not; if not active, he may not log in.

```python
class LoginForm(Form):
    def get_user(self):
        return User.query.filter_by(username=self.username.data).first()

    user = property(get_user)

    username = StringField(validators=
        [validators.InputRequired()])
    password = PasswordField(validators=
        [validators.InputRequired()])
```

```
def validate_username(self, field):
    "Validates that the username belongs to an actual user"
    if self.user is None:
        # do not send a very specific error message here,
            otherwise you'll
        # be telling the user which users are available in
            your database
        raise ValidationError('Your username and password did
            not match')

def validate_password(self, field):
    username = field.data
    user = User.query.get(username)

    if user is not None:
        if not user.password == field.data:
            raise ValidationError('Your username and password
                did not match')
```

Here we write the `LoginForm` ourselves. You could say: "Why not use `model_form`, dude?" Well, to use `model_form` here, you would have to initialize your database with your app (that you do not have yet) and set up a context. Just too much trouble.

We also define two custom validators, one to check if the `username` is valid and another to check if the `password` and `username` match.

> Notice we give very broad error messages for this particular form. We do this in order to avoid giving too much info to a possible attacker.

```
class Config(object):
    "Base configuration class"
    DEBUG = False
    SECRET_KEY = 'secret'
    SQLALCHEMY_DATABASE_URI = 'sqlite:////tmp/ex03.db'


class Dev(Config):
    "Our dev configuration"
    DEBUG = True
    SQLALCHEMY_DATABASE_URI = 'sqlite:////tmp/dev.db'


def setup(app):
    # initializing our extensions ; )
```

```
    db.init_app(app)
    principal.init_app(app)
    login_manager.init_app(app)

    # adding views without using decorators
    app.add_url_rule('/admin/', view_func=admin_view)
    app.add_url_rule('/admin/context/', view_func=admin_only_view)
    app.add_url_rule('/login/', view_func=login_view,
      methods=['GET', 'POST'])
    app.add_url_rule('/logout/', view_func=logout_view)

    # connecting on_identity_loaded signal to our app
    # you may also connect using the
      @identity_loaded.connect_via(app) decorator
    identity_loaded.connect(on_identity_loaded, app, False)


# our application factory
def app_factory(name=__name__, config=Dev):
    app = Flask(name)
    app.config.from_object(config)
    setup(app)
    return app
```

Here we define our configuration objects, our `app` setup, and application factory. I would say the tricky part is the setup, as it registers views using an `app` method and not a decorator (yes, the same result as using `@app.route`) and we connect our `identity_loaded` signal to our app, so that the user identity is loaded and available in each request. We could also register it as a decorator, like this:

```
@identity_loaded.connect_via(app)

# we use the decorator to let the login_manager know of our load_user
# userid is the model id attribute by default
@login_manager.user_loader
def load_user(userid):
    """

    Loads an user using the user_id

    Used by flask-login to load the user with the user id stored in
session
    """
    return User.query.get(userid)

def on_identity_loaded(sender, identity):
    # Set the identity user object
    identity.user = current_user
```

```
    # in case you have resources that belong to a specific user
    if hasattr(current_user, 'id'):
        identity.provides.add(UserNeed(current_user.id))

    # Assuming the User model has a list of roles, update the
    # identity with the roles that the user provides
    if hasattr(current_user, 'roles'):
        for role in current_user.roles:
            identity.provides.add(RoleNeed(role.name))
```

The `load_user` function is required by Flask-Login to load the user using the `userid` stored in the session storage. It should return `None`, if the `userid` was not found. Do not throw an exception here.

`on_identity_loaded` is registered with the `identity_loaded` signal and is used to load identity needs stored in your models. This is required because Flask-Principal is a generic solution and has no idea of how you have your permissions stored.

```
def login_view():
    form = LoginForm()

    if form.validate_on_submit():
        # authenticate the user...
        login_user(form.user)

        # Tell Flask-Principal the identity changed
        identity_changed.send(
            # do not use current_app directly
            current_app._get_current_object(),
            identity=Identity(form.user.id))
        flash("Logged in successfully.")
        return redirect(request.args.get("next") or
            url_for("admin_view"))

    return render_template("login.html", form=form)


@login_required  # you can't logout if you're not logged
def logout_view():
    # Remove the user information from the session
    # Flask-Login can handle this on its own = ]
    logout_user()

    # Remove session keys set by Flask-Principal
    for key in ('identity.name', 'identity.auth_type'):
        session.pop(key, None)
```

```
    # Tell Flask-Principal the user is anonymous
    identity_changed.send(
        current_app._get_current_object(),
        identity=AnonymousIdentity())

    # it's good practice to redirect after logout
    return redirect(request.args.get('next') or '/')
```

login_view and logout_view are just what is expected of them: a view to authenticate and another to unauthenticate the user. In both cases, you just have to make sure to call the appropriate Flask-Login functions (login_user and logout_user) and send an adequate Flask-Principal signal (and clean the session in the logout).

```
    # I like this approach better ...
    @login_required
    @admin_permission.require()
    def admin_view():
        """
        Only admins can access this
        """
        return render_template('admin.html')


    # Meh ...
    @login_required
    def admin_only_view():
        """
        Only admins can access this
        """
        with admin_permission.require():
            # using context
            return render_template('admin.html')
```

Finally, we have our actual views: admin_view and admin_only_view. Both of them do the exact same thing, they check whether the user is logged with Flask-Login and then check if they have adequate permission to access the view. The difference here is that, in the first scenario, admin_view uses permission as a decorator to verify the user's credentials and as a context in the second scenario.

```
    def populate():
        """
        Populates our database with a single user, for testing ; )

        Why not use fixtures? Just don't wanna ...
        """
```

```
        user = User(username='student', password='passwd',
            active=True)
        db.session.add(user)
        db.session.commit()
        role = Role(name='admin', user_id=user.id)
        db.session.add(role)
        db.session.commit()


if __name__ == '__main__':
    app = app_factory()

    # we need to use a context here, otherwise we'll get a runtime
error
    with app.test_request_context():
        db.drop_all()
        db.create_all()
        populate()

    app.run()
```

`populate` is used to add a proper user and role to our database in case you want to test it.

A word of caution about our earlier example: we used plain text for the user database. In actual live code, you don't want to do that because it is common practice for users to use the same password for multiple sites. If the password is in plain text, anyone with access to the database will be able know it and test it against sensitive sites. The solution provided in `http://flask.pocoo.org/snippets/54/` might help you avoid this scenario.

Now here is an example `base.html` template you could use with the preceding code:

```
<!doctype html>
<html lang="en">
<head>
  <meta charset="UTF-8">
  <title>{% block title %}{% endblock %}</title>

  <link rel="stylesheet" media="screen,projection"
    href="https://cdnjs.cloudflare.com/ajax/libs/materialize/0.96.1/
css/materialize.min.css" />
```

```
    <meta name="viewport" content="width=device-width, initial-
      scale=1.0, maximum-scale=1.0, user-scalable=no"/>
    <style type="text/css">
      .messages{
        position: fixed;
        list-style: none;
        margin:0px;
        padding: .5rem 2rem;
        bottom: 0; left: 0;
        width:100%;
        background-color: #abc;
        text-align: center;
      }
    </style>
</head>
<body>
    {% with messages = get_flashed_messages() %}
      {% if messages %}
      <ul class='messages'>
          {% for message in messages %}
          <li>{{ message }}</li>
          {% endfor %}
      </ul>
      {% endif %}
    {% endwith %}

    <header>
       <nav>
        <div class="container nav-wrapper">
           {% if current_user.is_authenticated() %}
           <span>Welcome to the admin interface, {{
             current_user.username }}</span>
           {% else %}<span>Welcome, stranger</span>{% endif %}

           <ul id="nav-mobile" class="right hide-on-med-and-down">
             {% if current_user.is_authenticated() %}
             <li><a href="{{ url_for('logout_view')
               }}?next=/admin/">Logout</a></li>
             {% else %}
             <li><a href="{{ url_for('login_view')
               }}?next=/admin/">Login</a></li>
             {% endif %}
           </ul>
         </div>
       </nav>
```

```
    </header>
    <div class="container">
      {% block content %}{% endblock %}
    </div>
    <script type="text/javascript"
      src="https://code.jquery.com/jquery-2.1.1.min.js"></script>
    <script src="https://cdnjs.cloudflare.com/ajax/
      libs/materialize/0.96.1/js/materialize.min.js"></script>
  </body>
</html>
```

Notice we use `current_user.is_authenticated()` to check if the user is authenticated in the template as `current_user` is available in all templates. Now, try writing `login.html` and `admin.html` on your own, extending `base.html`.

Admin like a boss

One of the reasons why Django got so famous is because it has a nice and flexible administrative interface and we want one too!

Just like Flask-Principal and Flask-Login, Flask-Admin, the extension we'll use to build our administrative interface, does not require a particular database to work with. You may use MongoDB as a relational database (with SQLAlchemy or PeeWee), or another database you happen to like.

Contrary to Django, where the admin interface is focused in the apps/models, Flask-Admin is focused in page/models. You cannot (without some heavy coding) load a whole blueprint (the Flask equivalent of a Django app) into the admin interface, but you can create a page for your blueprint and register the blueprint models with it. One advantage of this approach is that you may pick where all your models will be listed with ease.

In our previous example, we created two models to hold our user and role information, so, let's create a simple admin interface for these two models. We make sure our dependency is installed:

pip install flask-admin

And then:

```
# coding:utf-8

from flask import Flask
from flask.ext.admin import Admin
from flask.ext.admin.contrib.sqla import ModelView
from flask.ext.login import UserMixin
```

```
from flask.ext.sqlalchemy import SQLAlchemy


db = SQLAlchemy()


class User(db.Model, UserMixin):
    __tablename__ = 'users'

    id = db.Column(db.Integer, primary_key=True)
    active = db.Column(db.Boolean, default=False)
    username = db.Column(db.String(60), unique=True,
      nullable=False)
    password = db.Column(db.String(20), nullable=False)
    roles = db.relationship(
        'Role', backref='roles', lazy='dynamic')

    def __unicode__(self):
        return self.username

    # flask login expects an is_active method in your user model
    # you usually inactivate a user account if you don't want it
    # to have access to the system anymore
    def is_active(self):
        """
        Tells flask-login if the user account is active
        """
        return self.active


class Role(db.Model):
    """
    Holds our user roles
    """
    __tablename__ = 'roles'
    name = db.Column(db.String(60), primary_key=True)
    user_id = db.Column(db.Integer, db.ForeignKey('users.id'))

    def __unicode__(self):
        return self.name

# Flask and Flask-SQLAlchemy initialization here
admin = Admin()
admin.add_view(ModelView(User, db.session, category='Profile'))
admin.add_view(ModelView(Role, db.session, category='Profile'))
```

```
def app_factory(name=__name__):
    app = Flask(name)
    app.debug = True
    app.config['SECRET_KEY'] = 'secret'
    app.config['SQLALCHEMY_DATABASE_URI'] =
      'sqlite:////tmp/ex04.db'

    db.init_app(app)
    admin.init_app(app)
    return app


if __name__ == '__main__':
    app = app_factory()

    # we need to use a context here, otherwise we'll get a runtime
error
    with app.test_request_context():
        db.drop_all()
        db.create_all()

    app.run()
```

In this example, we create and initialize the `admin` extension and then register our models with it using `ModelView`, a special class that creates a **CRUD** for our model. Run this code and try to access `http://127.0.0.1:5000/admin/`; you'll see a nice administrative interface with a Home link at the top followed by a Profile drop-down with two links, **User** and **Role**, that point to our model CRUDs. That's a very basic example that does not amount to much, as you cannot have an administrative interface like that, open to all users.

One way to add authentication and permission verification to our admin views is by extending `ModelView` and `IndexView`. We'll also use a cool design pattern called `mixin`:

```
# coding:utf-8
# permissions.py

from flask.ext.principal import RoleNeed, UserNeed, Permission
from flask.ext.principal import Principal

principal = Principal()

# admin permission role
admin_permission = Permission(RoleNeed('admin'))

# END of FILE
```

```
# coding:utf-8
# admin.py

from flask import g
from flask.ext.login import current_user, login_required
from flask.ext.admin import Admin, AdminIndexView, expose
from flask.ext.admin.contrib.sqla import ModelView

from permissions import *


class AuthMixinView(object):
    def is_accessible(self):
        has_auth = current_user.is_authenticated()
        has_perm = admin_permission.allows(g.identity)
        return has_auth and has_perm


class AuthModelView(AuthMixinView, ModelView):
    @expose()
    @login_required
    def index_view(self):
        return super(ModelView, self).index_view()


class AuthAdminIndexView(AuthMixinView, AdminIndexView):
    @expose()
    @login_required
    def index_view(self):
        return super(AdminIndexView, self).index_view()

admin = Admin(name='Administrative Interface',
    index_view=AuthAdminIndexView())
```

What are we doing here? We overwrite the `is_accessible` method, so that users without permission will receive a forbidden-access message, and overwrite the `index_view` for `AdminIndexView` and `ModelView`, adding the `login_required` decorator that will redirect unauthenticated users to the login page. `admin_permission` verifies that the given identity has the required set of permissions—`RoleNeed('admin')`, in our case.

 If you're wondering what a mixin is, try this link
`http://stackoverflow.com/questions/533631/`
`what-is-a-mixin-and-why-are-they-useful`.

As our model already has **Create, Read, Update, Delete (CRUD)** and permission control access, how could we modify our CRUD to show just certain fields, or prevent the addition of other fields?

Just like Django Admin, Flask-Admin allows you to change your ModelView behavior through setting class attributes. A few of my personal favorites are these:

- `can_create`: This allows the user to create the model using CRUD.
- `can_edit`: This allows the user to update the model using CRUD.
- `can_delete`: This allows the user to delete the model using CRUD.
- `list_template`, `edit_template`, and `create_template`: These are default CRUD templates.
- `list_columns`: This implies thats columns show in the list view.
- `column_editable_list`: This indicates columns that can be edited in the list view.
- `form`: This is the form used by CRUD to edit and create views.
- `form_args`: This is used to pass form field arguments. Use it like this:
  ```
  form_args = {'form_field_name': {'parameter': 'value'}}  #
  parameter could be name, for example
  ```
- `form_overrides`: use it to override a form field like this:
  ```
  form_overrides = {'form_field': wtforms.SomeField}
  ```
- `form_choices`: allow you to define choices for a form field. Use it like this:
  ```
  form_choices = {'form_field': [('value store in db', 'value
  display in the combo box')]}
  ```

An example would look like this:

```
class AuthModelView(AuthMixinView, ModelView):
    can_edit= False
    form = MyAuthForm

    @expose()
    @login_required
    def index_view(self):
        return super(ModelView, self).index_view()
```

Custom pages

Now, were you willing to add a custom **reports page** to your administrative interface, you certainly would not use a model view for the task. For these cases, add a custom `BaseView` like this:

```
# coding:utf-8
from flask import Flask
from flask.ext.admin import Admin, BaseView, expose


class ReportsView(BaseView):
    @expose('/')
    def index(self):
        # make sure reports.html exists
        return self.render('reports.html')


app = Flask(__name__)
admin = Admin(app)
admin.add_view(ReportsView(name='Reports Page'))

if __name__ == '__main__':
    app.debug = True
    app.run()
```

Now you have an admin interface with a nice Reports Page link at the top. Do not forget to write a `reports.html` page in order to make the preceding example work.

Now, what if you don't want the link to be shown in the navigation bar, because you have it somewhere else? Overwrite the `BaseView.is_visible` method as it controls whether the view will appear in the navigation bar. Do it like this:

```
class ReportsView(BaseView):
...
  def is_visible(self):
    return False
```

Summary

In this chapter, we just learned some tricks with regard to user authorization and authentication, and even had a go at creating an administrative interface. That was quite a lot of knowledge that will help you extensively in your daily coding, as security (and making sure people just interact with what they can and should interact with) is a quite common need.

Rejoice, my friend, as now you know how to develop robust Flask applications, using MVC, TDD, relational, and NoSQL databases integrated with permissions and authentication control: forms; how to implement cross site forgery protection; and even how to use an administrative tool out-of-the-box.

The focus of our studies was on knowing all the most useful tools (in my opinion, of course) in the Flask development world and how to use them to some extent. We did not explore any of them in greater depth, because of scope restrictions, but the basics were certainly shown.

Now, it is left for you to improve your understanding of each of the presented extensions and libraries and to for new ones. The next and final chapter tries to enlighten you in this journey, suggesting reading material, articles, and tutorials (among other things).

I hope you've enjoyed the book so far and take great pleasure in the final notes.

10
What Now?

Flask is quite the most popular Web framework nowadays, so finding online reading material for it is not that hard. For instance, a quick search on Google will surely give you one or two good articles on most subjects you might be interested in. Nonetheless, subjects such as deployment, even though much discussed on the Internet, yet raise doubt in our fellow web warriors' hearts. For that reason, we have stashed a nice step-by-step "deploy your Flask app like a boss" recipe in our last chapter. Along with it, we'll advise you on a few very special places where knowledge is just there, thick and juicy, lying around waiting for you to pinch wisdom. With this chapter, you'll be capable of delivering your products from code to server, and maybe, just maybe, fetching some well-deserved high fives! Welcome to this chapter, where code meets the server and you meet the world!

You deploy better than my ex

Deployment is not a term everyone is familiar with; if you were not a web developer until recently, you would have been, probably, unfamiliar with it. In a rough Spartan way, one could define deployment as the act of preparing and presenting your application to the world, assuring the required resources are available, and tuning it, as a configuration suitable for the development phase is not the same as one appropriate for deployment. In a web development context, we are talking about a few very specific actions:

- Placing your code in a server
- Setting up your database
- Setting up your HTTP server
- Setting up other services you may use
- Tying everything together

Placing your code in a server

First of all, what is a server? We refer to as server a computer with server-like features such as high reliability, availability, and serviceability (**RAS**). These features grant the application running in the server a certain level of trust that the server will keep running, even after any environment problem, such as a hardware failure.

In the real world, where people have budgets, a normal computer (one of those you buy in the closest store) would most likely be the best choice for running a small application because "real servers" are very expensive. With small project budgets (nowadays, also the big ones), a robust solution called server virtualization was created where expensive, high-RAS physical servers have their resources (memory, CPU, hard-drive, and so on) virtualized into **virtual machines** (**VM**), which act just like smaller (and cheaper) versions of the real hardware. Companies such as DigitalOcean (https://digitalocean.com/), Linode (https://www.linode.com/), and RamNode (https://www.ramnode.com/) have whole businesses focused in providing cheap, reliable virtual machines to the public.

Now, given that we have our web application ready (I mean, our Minimum Viable Product is ready), we must run the code somewhere accessible to our target audience. This usually means we need a web server. Pick two cheap virtual machines from one of the companies mentioned in the preceding paragraph, set up with Ubuntu, and let's begin!

Setting up your database

With respect to databases, one of the most basic things you should know during deployment is that it is a good practice to have your database and web application running on different (virtual) machines. You don't want them to compete for the same resources, believe me. That's why we hired two virtual servers—one will run our HTTP server and the other our database.

Let's begin our database server setup; first, we add our SSH credentials to our remote server so that we may authenticate without the need to type the remote server user password every time. Before this, generate your SSH keys if you do not have them, like this:

```
# ref: https://help.github.com/articles/generating-ssh-keys/
# type a passphrase when asked for one
ssh-keygen -t rsa -b 4096 -C "your_email@example.com"
```

Now, given that your virtual machine provider provided you with an IP address to your remote machine, a root user, and password, we create a passwordless SSH authentication with our server as follows:

```
# type the root password when requested
ssh-copy-id root@ipaddress
```

Now, exit your remote terminal and try to SSH root@ipaddress. The password will no longer be requested.

Here's the second step! Get rid of the non-database stuff such as Apache and install Postgres (http://www.postgresql.org/), the most advanced open source database to date:

```
# as root
apt-get purge apache2-*
apt-get install postgresql
# type to check which version of postgres was installed (most likely 9.x)
psql -V
```

Now we set up the database.

Connect the default user Postgres with the role postgres:

```
sudo -u postgres psql
```

Create a database for our project called mydb:

```
CREATE DATABASE mydb;
```

Create a new user role to access our database:

```
CREATE USER you WITH PASSWORD 'passwd'; # please, use a strong password

# We now make sure "you" can do whatever you want with mydb
# You don't want to keep this setup for long, be warned
GRANT ALL PRIVILEGES ON DATABASE mydb TO you;
```

So far, we've accomplished quite a lot. First, we removed unnecessary packages (just a few); installed the latest supported version of our database, Postgres; created a new database and a new "user"; and granted full permissions to our user over our new database. Let's understand each step.

We begin by removing Apache2 and the likes because this is a database server setup and so there is no need to keep the Apache2 packages. Depending on the installed Ubuntu version, you will even need to remove other packages as well. The golden rule here is: the fewer packages installed, the fewer packages we have to pay attention to. Keep only the minimum.

Then we install Postgres. Depending on your background, you might ask — Why Postgres and why not MariaDB/MySQL? Well, well, fellow reader, Postgres is a complete solution with ACID support, document (JSONB) storage, key-value storage (with HStore), indexing, text searching, server-side programming, geolocalization (with PostGIS), and so on. If you know how to install and use Postgres, you have access to all these functionalities in a single solution. I also like it more than other open source/free solutions, so we'll stick with it.

After installing Postgres, we have to configure it. Unlike SQLite, which we have used so far as our relational database solution, Postgres has a robust permissions system based on roles that controls which resources may be accessed or modified, and by whom. The main concept here is that roles are a very particular kind of group, which may have permissions called **privileges**, or other groups associated with or containing it. For example, the command CREATE USER run inside the psql console (the Postgres interactive console, just like Python's) is not actually creating a user; it is, in reality, creating a new role with the login privilege, which is similar to the user concept. The following command is equivalent to the create user command inside psql:

```
CREATE ROLE you WITH LOGIN;
```

Now, toward our last sphinx, there is the GRANT command. To allow roles to do stuff, we grant them privileges, such as the login privilege that allows our "user" to log in. In our example, we grant you all available privileges to the database mydb. We do that so that we're able to create tables, alter tables, and so on. You usually don't want your production web application database user (whoa!) to have all these privileges because, in the event of a security breach, the invader would be able to do anything to your database. As one usually (coff coff never!) does not alter the database structure on user interaction, using a less privileged user with the web application is not a problem.

 PgAdmin is an amazing, user-friendly, Postgres management application. Just use it with SSH tunneling (http://www.pgadmin.org/docs/dev/connect.html), and be happy!

Now test that your database setup is working. Connect to it from the console:

```
psql -U user_you -d database_mydb -h 127.0.0.1 -W
```

Enter your password when asked for it. Our preceding command is actually a trick we use with Postgres as we are connecting to the database through a network interface. By default, Postgres assumes you're trying to connect with a role and database of the same name as your system username. You cannot even connect as a role whose name is different than your system username, unless you do it from a network interface as we did.

Setting up the web server

Setting up your web server is a little more complex as it involves modifying more files and making sure the configuration is solid across them, but we'll make it, you'll see.

First, we make sure our project code is in our web server (that is not the same server as the database server, right?). We may do this in one of many ways: using FTP (please don't), plain fabric plus rsync, version control, or version plus fabric (happy face!). Let's see how to do the latter.

Given you already created a regular user in your web server virtual machine called `myuser`, make sure you have fabric installed:

```
sudo apt-get install python-dev
pip install fabric
```

And, a file called `fabfile.py` in your project root:

```python
# coding:utf-8

from fabric.api import *
from fabric.contrib.files import exists

env.linewise = True
# forward_agent allows you to git pull from your repository
# if you have your ssh key setup
env.forward_agent = True
env.hosts = ['your.host.ip.address']


def create_project():
    if not exists('~/project'):
        run('git clone git://path/to/repo.git')


def update_code():
    with cd('~/project'):
        run('git pull')
def reload():
    "Reloads project instance"
    run('touch --no-dereference /tmp/reload')
```

With the preceding code and fabric installed, given you have your SSH key copied to the remote server with `ssh-copy-id` and have it set up with your version control provider (for example, `github` or `bitbucket`), `create_project` and `update_code` become available to you. You may use them, like this:

```
fab create_project  # creates our project in the home folder of our
remote web server
fab update_code  # updates our project code from the version control
repository
```

It's very easy. The first command gets your code in the repository, while the second updates it to your last commit.

Our web server setup will use some very popular tools:

- **uWSGI**: This is used for application server and process management
- **Nginx**: This is used as our HTTP server
- **UpStart**: This is used to manage our uWSGI life cycle

UpStart comes with Ubuntu out-of-the-box, so we'll remember it for later. For uWSGI, we need to install it, like this:

```
pip install uwsgi
```

Now, inside your virtualenv `bin` folder, there will be a uWSGI command. Keep track of where it is as we'll need it soon.

Create a `wsgi.py` file inside your project folder with the following content:

```
# coding:utf-8
from main import app_factory

app = app_factory(name="myproject")
```

A uWSGI uses the app instance from the file above to connect to our application. An `app_factory` is a factory function that creates our application. We have seen a few so far. Just make sure the app instance it returns is properly configured. Application-wise, this is all we have to do. Next, we move on to connecting uWSGI to our application.

We may call our uWSGI binary with all the parameters necessary to load our wsgi. py file directly from command line or we can create an `ini` file, with all the necessary configuration, and just provide it to the binary. As you may guess, the second approach is usually better, so create an ini file that looks like this:

```
[uwsgi]
user-home = /home/your-system-username
project-name = myproject
```

```
project-path = %(user-home)/%(myproject)

# make sure paths exist
socket = %(user-home)/%(project-name).sock
pidfile = %(user-home)/%(project-name).pid
logto = /var/tmp/uwsgi.%(prj).log
touch-reload = /tmp/reload
chdir = %(project-path)
wsgi-file = %(project-path)/wsgi.py
callable = app
chmod-socket = 664

master = true
processes = 5
vacuum = true
die-on-term = true
optimize = 2
```

The user-home, project-name, and project-path are aliases we use to make our work easier. The socket option points to the socket file our HTTP server will use to communicate with our application. We'll not discuss all the given options as this is not an overview on uWSGI, but a few more important options, such as touch-reload, wsgi-file, callable, and chmod-socket, will receive a detailed explanation. Touch-reload is particularly useful; the file you specify as an argument to it will be watched by uWSGI and, whenever it is updated/touched, your application will be reloaded. After some code update, you certainly want to reload your app. Wsgi-file specifies which file has our WSGI-compatible application, while callable tells uWSGI the name of the instance in the wsgi file (app, usually). Finally, we have chmod-socket, which changes our socket permission to -rw-rw-r--, aka read/write permission to the owner and group; others may but read this. We need this as we want our application in the user scope and our sockets to be read from the www-data user, which is the server user. This setup is quite secure as the application cannot mess with anything beyond the system user resources.

We may now set up our HTTP server, which is quite an easy step. Just install Nginx as follows:

```
sudo apt-get install nginx-full
```

Now, your http server is up-and-running on port 80. Let's make sure Nginx knows about our application. Write the following code to a file called project inside /etc/nginx/sites-available:

```
server {
    listen 80;
    server_name PROJECT_DOMAIN;
```

```
    location /media {
        alias /path/to/media;
    }
    location /static {
        alias /path/to/static;
    }

    location / {
        include         /etc/nginx/uwsgi_params;
        uwsgi_pass      unix:/path/to/socket/file.sock;
    }
}
```

The preceding configuration file creates a virtual server running at port 80, listening to the domain server_name, serving static and media files from the provided paths through /static and /media, and listening to the path directing all access to / to be handled using our socket. We now turn on our configuration and turn off the default configuration for nginx:

```
sudo rm /etc/nginx/sites-enabled/default

ln -s /etc/nginx/sites-available/project /etc/nginx/sites-enabled/project
```

What have we just done? The configuration files for virtual servers live inside /etc/nginx/sites-available/ and, whenever we want a configuration to be seen by nginx, we symlink it to the enabled sites. In the preceding configuration, we just disabled default and enabled project by symlinking it. Nginx does not notice and load what we just did on its own; we need to tell it to reload its configuration. Let's save this step for later.

We need to create one last file inside /etc/init that will register our uWSGI process as a service with upstart. This part is really easy; just create a file called project.conf (or any other meaningful name) with the following content:

```
description "uWSGI application my project"

start on runlevel [2345]
stop on runlevel [!2345]

setuid your-user
setgid www-data

exec /path/to/uwsgi --ini /path/to/ini/file.ini
```

The preceding script runs uWSGI using our project `ini` file (we created it earlier) as parameter as the user "your-user" and group www-data. Replace `your-user` with your user (…) but, do not replace the `www-data` group as it is a required configuration. The preceding runlevel configuration just tells upstart when to start and stop this service. You don't have to intervene.

Run the following command line to start your service:

```
start project
```

Next reload Nginx configuration like this:

```
sudo /etc/init.d/nginx reload
```

If everything went fine, the media path and static path exist, the project database settings point to the remote server inside the private network, and the gods are smiling on you, your project should be accessible from your registered domain. Gimme a high-five!!

StackOverflow

StackOverflow is the new Google term for hacking and software development. A lot of people use it, so there are a lot of common questions and great answers at your disposal. Just spend a few hours reading the latest trends on `http://stackoverflow.com/search?q=flask`, and you're sure to have learned much!

Structuring your projects

As Flask does not enforce a project structure, you've quite a lot of freedom to try out what best suits you. Large one-file projects work, Django-like structured projects work, flat architectures also work; the possibilities are many! Because of this, many projects emerge with their own suggested architecture; these projects are called boilerplates or skeletons. They focus on giving you a recipe to quickly start a new Flask project, taking advantage of their suggested way of organizing the code.

If you plan to create a large web application with Flask, you're strongly advised to take a look at at least one of these projects because they've probably already faced a few problems you could face and have come up with a solution:

- Flask-Empty (`https://github.com/italomaia/flask-empty`)
- Flask-Boilerplate (`https://github.com/mbr/flask-bootstrap`)
- Flask-Skeleton (`https://github.com/sean-/flask-skeleton`)

Summary

I must confess, I wrote this book for myself. It is so hard to find all the knowledge one needs to build a web application in just one place, that I had to place my notes somewhere, condensed. I hope that, if you reached this paragraph, you also feel like me, that this book was written for you. It was a nice challenging ride.

You're now capable of building full-featured Flask applications with secure forms, database integration, tests, and making use of extensions, which allow you to create robust software in no time. I'm so proud! Now, go tell your friends how awesome you are. See you around!

Postscript

As a personal challenge, take that project you have always dreamed of coding, but never had the spirit to do it, and make an MVP (minimum viable product) of it. Create a very simple implementation of your idea and publish it (`http://bit.ly/1I0ehDB`) to the world to see; then, leave me a message about it. I'd love to take a look at your work!

Index

H

"Hello World" app
  about 5
  creating 6-8
HTML
  about 27
  reference link 27
HTML forms
  about 27-29
  example 28
HTML pages
  serving 9, 10
HTTP
  about 58
  DELETE method 58
  GET method 58
  OPTIONS method 58
  POST method 58
  PUT method 58

I

if statement 16
include statement 18, 19
input field
  reference link 29
integration testing 84

J

JavaScript
  reference link 51
Jinja2
  about 11, 12
  control structures 15-20
  extensions 22, 23
  filters 23, 24
  macros 20-22
  template context, modifying 25
  URL 11
  using 12-15
JSON
  reference link 51

L

lettuce

URL 74
Light Table editor
  URL 6
Linode
  URL 122
LiveServer 77-80
logging
  about 94
  example 94, 95
  purpose 96

M

macros
  about 20, 21
  advantages 22
Mint
  URL 5
mixin
  reference link 117
MongoDB
  about 50
  example 51
  Flask-MongoEngine 54-56
  installing 51
  MongoEngine 52, 53
  rules 52
MongoEngine
  about 52
  example 53
  installing 52
  reference link 53
MVC 39
MxN relationship 40

N

Nginx
  using 126
normal forms
  reference link 41
NoSQL database
  about 39
  versus relational database 56

O

Oracle 42

overengineering 86

P

PgAdmin
  about 124
  URL 124
PhantomJS
  about 76, 77
  URL 77
Postgres
  URL, for installing 123
premature optimization 86
primary key 40
privileges 124
projects
  structuring 129
pseudo-random data 81
PyCharm IDE
  about 85
  URL 6
PyMongo 52
Python 2.x 5

R

RamNode
  URL 122
regular expressions (Regex)
  references 12
relational database
  about 39
  versus NoSQL database 56
REST
  about 57
  references 57
RESTful Web Service API
  about 57
  data, recording to database 64, 65
  example 58-63
rows 40

S

Selenium 76
server
  about 122
  code, placing 122

sessions
  about 99
  example 101
  using 101
set statement 20
software quality 69
SQL
  about 39
  reference link 40
SQLAlchemy
  about 40
  concepts 40, 41
  example 42-47
  Flask-SQLAlchemy 48-50
  installing 41
  reference link 47
SQL Injection Attack 50
SQLite
  about 40
  URL 40
StackOverflow
  about 129
  URL 129

T

tables 40
tags 27
template context
  modifying 25
Test Driven Development (TDD) 70
tests
  about 70
  black-box tests 70
  white-box tests 70
tools
  using 5, 6
transactions 40-42

U

Ubuntu
  URL 5
unit 70
unit testing
  about 70
  example 71-74

Thank you for buying
Building Web Applications with Flask

About Packt Publishing

Packt, pronounced 'packed', published its first book, *Mastering phpMyAdmin for Effective MySQL Management*, in April 2004, and subsequently continued to specialize in publishing highly focused books on specific technologies and solutions.

Our books and publications share the experiences of your fellow IT professionals in adapting and customizing today's systems, applications, and frameworks. Our solution-based books give you the knowledge and power to customize the software and technologies you're using to get the job done. Packt books are more specific and less general than the IT books you have seen in the past. Our unique business model allows us to bring you more focused information, giving you more of what you need to know, and less of what you don't.

Packt is a modern yet unique publishing company that focuses on producing quality, cutting-edge books for communities of developers, administrators, and newbies alike. For more information, please visit our website at www.packtpub.com.

About Packt Open Source

In 2010, Packt launched two new brands, Packt Open Source and Packt Enterprise, in order to continue its focus on specialization. This book is part of the Packt Open Source brand, home to books published on software built around open source licenses, and offering information to anybody from advanced developers to budding web designers. The Open Source brand also runs Packt's Open Source Royalty Scheme, by which Packt gives a royalty to each open source project about whose software a book is sold.

Writing for Packt

We welcome all inquiries from people who are interested in authoring. Book proposals should be sent to author@packtpub.com. If your book idea is still at an early stage and you would like to discuss it first before writing a formal book proposal, then please contact us; one of our commissioning editors will get in touch with you.

We're not just looking for published authors; if you have strong technical skills but no writing experience, our experienced editors can help you develop a writing career, or simply get some additional reward for your expertise.

PUBLISHING

Rapid Flask
Gareth Dwyer

[PACKT]▶

Rapid Flask [Video]

ISBN: 978-1-78355-425-6   Duration: 00:42 hours

Get your web applications up and running in no time with Flask

1. Build a web app using Flask from beginning to end – never touch PHP again!.

2. Not just "hello, world"- create a fully functional web app that includes web services, HTML forms, and more.

3. Your apps won't look like they came out of the '90s – learn how to integrate basic styles and icons.

4. Go further – Get a glimpse of how to utilize Flask's more popular extensions.

Quick answers to common problems

Flask Framework Cookbook

Over 80 hands-on recipes to help you create small-to-large web applications using Flask

Shalabh Aggarwal   [   ] open source

Flask Framework Cookbook

ISBN: 978-1-78398-340-7   Paperback: 258 pages

Over 80 hands-on recipes to help you create small-to-large web applications using Flask

1. Get the most out of the powerful Flask framework while remaining flexible with your design choices.

2. Build end-to-end web applications, right from their installation to the post-deployment stages.

3. Packed with recipes containing lots of sample applications to help you understand the intricacies of the code.

Please check **www.PacktPub.com** for information on our titles

Instant Flask Web Development

ISBN: 978-1-78216-962-8   Paperback: 78 pages

Tap into Flask to build a complete application in a style that you control

1. Learn something new in an Instant! A short, fast, focused guide delivering immediate results.

2. Build a small but complete web application with Python and Flask.

3. Explore the basics of web page layout using Twitter Bootstrap and jQuery.

4. Get to know how to validate data entry using HTML forms and WTForms.

Web Development with Django Cookbook

ISBN: 978-1-78328-689-8   Paperback: 294 pages

Over 70 practical recipes to create multilingual, responsive, and scalable websites with Django

1. Improve your skills by developing models, forms, views, and templates.

2. Create a rich user experience using Ajax and other JavaScript techniques.

3. A practical guide to writing and using APIs to import or export data.

Please check **www.PacktPub.com** for information on our titles